DENIAL, CONFRONTATION, OBSESSION AND RETURN

Four Short Plays

Maria Teresa H. de Holcomb

Copyright © 2015 Maria Teresa H. de Holcomb
All rights reserved.

ISBN: 1512358630
ISBN 13: 9781512358636
Library of Congress Control Number: 2015908716
CreateSpace Independent Publishing Platform
North Charleston, South Carolina

To my husband,
the wonderful young man I met in college many years ago

CONTENTS

A Family in Denial..1
A Tale of Three Selfies 51
Together for Eternity...111
A Return to the Beginning.......................................145

A Family in Denial

CHARACTERS

WILLIAM, a father in his late thirties
ARLENE, a mother in her midthirties
BETTY, their daughter, thirteen years old
DEANA, their daughter, eleven years old
PEDIATRICIAN, midfifties
PSYCHIATRIST, midsixties

LOCATION

Denver, Colorado

TIME

Present day

ACT I

Scene 1

Lights rise. William, Arlene, Betty, and Deana are sitting at a dining-room table.

ARLENE
(*irritated*)
William, why do you always promise to take me shopping, and then you cancel the plans because you have to work? That is unfair. You are selfish!

WILLIAM
(*pounds the table with his fist*)
Arlene, I am forced to work extra hours because of the way you shop. Yes, yes, to pay for your extravagant shopping trips.

ARLENE
Well, my girlfriends' husbands have the skills to bring in the money and to be considerate to the needs of their wives.

WILLIAM
I am not like their husbands. They are wimps.

ARLENE
If they are wimps, then maybe you are a male chauvinist… (*She looks at the children, who are quiet and have their heads bowed.*) And

you children, why are you kissing the plate?
Sit up straight!

WILLIAM
There you go again. If you are not attacking me, you are attacking the children. Maybe you should look at your own soul.

ARLENE
Well, at least I have one.

William stands up abruptly, walks toward his wife, and shakes his finger in her face.

WILLIAM
All you do is nag me and complain about the children.

He quickly leaves the dining room.

BETTY
(*timidly*)
Mommy, may we leave the table?

ARLENE
Yes, go on. Get out of here!

Betty and Deana leave the dining room quietly with their heads bowed.

Blackout.

DENIAL, CONFRONTATION, OBSESSION AND RETURN

Scene 2

Lights rise. The entire family is sitting in the living room.

          WILLIAM
Arlene, why didn't you pick up my shirts from the cleaners? I told you several days ago that I needed them. I have an important presentation at work.

          ARLENE
I forgot. I have so many things to do around the house. Do you ever forget anything?

          WILLIAM
Yes, but not as often as you do.

          ARLENE
Yes, yes, you do! I can tell you what you forget. You forget to say please, thank you, and that you care about me.

          WILLIAM
Yes, I love you, but sometimes…

          ARLENE
Sometimes what?

          WILLIAM
Let's not start bickering again. The children are…

> BETTY
> (*speaking softly*)
> Mom and Dad, I don't like to see you act that way.

> DEANA
> (*subdued voice*)
> Mommy, Daddy, I don't like to hear you talk like that.

> ARLENE
> (*looking at her husband*)
> Girls, your father is just impossible to live with. He makes me so mad that I can't stand it!

> BETTY
> But Mommy, we love both of you, and we want you to love each other. We want to see you in a good mood.

> DEANA
> We want to hear you and Daddy talking nicely to each other. It makes us sad when we hear you talking so cranky.

Blackout.

Scene 3

Lights rise. Betty and Deana play with Legos in the living room at stage left, and William and Arlene sit in the dining room toward stage right.

DENIAL, CONFRONTATION, OBSESSION AND RETURN

ARLENE
William, last week you called twice to tell me you would be late for dinner. I bet you are taking that floozy secretary out for happy hour.
You can be happy with her, but no, never happy with me!

WILLIAM
I wonder why.

He exits.

BETTY
My friends' parents talk nicely to each other. They even kiss. I have seen them. Why can't Mom and Dad be like that?

Blackout.

Scene 4

Lights rise. Arlene is in the dining room as Betty and Deana enter. Arlene sets down a covered dish.

ARLENE
Girls, dinner is served. I'll get your father.

She exits offstage while the girls take their seats.

BETTY
Let's be very polite. Maybe it is our fault that they argue. Also, let's not forget to close our mouths when we are eating, and we must place the napkins on our laps.

DEANA
OK, OK.

Arlene enters. William follows.

ARLENE
Sit down and eat!

The children sit hastily and bow their heads.

ARLENE
Why don't you talk to us?

DEANA
(*reluctantly*)
We have food in our mouths, and we don't want you to get angry.

WILLIAM
Tell me, Arlene, why should they talk to us? All we have to offer them is anger and sarcasm.

ARLENE
Shut up, William! Deana, lately you have been playing your music very loudly. What is going on?

DENIAL, CONFRONTATION, OBSESSION AND RETURN

> **WILLIAM**
> It is very simple. She does not want to hear you. Children, before you go to sleep, come and kiss us goodnight just like the old days.
>
> **BETTY**
> Mom and Dad, we love you.

Scene 5

A few hours later. Betty and Deana's bedroom is at stage left, lit dimly. The girls brush their hair, arrange stuffed animals, and read as if getting ready to sleep. A spotlight on stage right shows William and Arlene's bedroom. William waves a sheet of paper as the couple argue. Betty and Deana turn toward the sound of their voices, then intermittently look away.

> **WILLIAM**
> Look at this credit-card balance! All you do is nag and spend.
>
> **ARLENE**
> Yeah, yeah, and all you do is work. You never pay any attention to me.
>
> **WILLIAM**
> Yes, I work to pay your bills.
>
> **ARLENE**
> William, listen to me! Do you realize you spend more time with your computer than with me?

> WILLIAM
> The computer does not nag me.

A spotlight follows Betty as she leaves her room and crosses center stage to knock at her parents' bedroom door. The light dims on William and Arlene.

> BETTY
> Mom? Dad? May I come in?

She opens the door slightly. The light rises on William and Arlene, showing William's hands around Arlene's throat. She shoves at his chest and pushes him away.

Betty closes their door. The light dims on William and Arlene as she stumbles across center stage in a daze back to her and Deana's room. Light rises on the girls' bedroom.

> BETTY
> Deana, why did you turn off the lights? I cannot see.

> DEANA
> I didn't turn them off.

Betty grasps the air in front of her. Deana, frightened, crosses center stage to her parents' room at stage right. Deana knocks at their door. The lights remain dim on William and Arlene.

> DEANA
> Something is wrong with Betty!

DENIAL, CONFRONTATION, OBSESSION AND RETURN

> **WILLIAM'S VOICE**
> Arlene, I am going to leave you and never come back.
>
> **ARLENE'S VOICE**
> (screaming)
> What about the children?
>
> **WILLIAM'S VOICE**
> Haven't you heard of orphanages?

Deana claps her hands over her ears, shaking her head repeatedly. She rushes back across the stage to her and Betty's room, at stage left.

> **BETTY**
> Did you tell them? I am so scared that I cannot see!
>
> **DEANA**
> I heard them arguing, and they said something about putting us in an orphanage. I could not hear anything after that.

She pulls her hands away from her ears, then starts to cry.

> **DEANA**
> Betty, I know you're talking because your lips are moving. But I can't hear anything.
>
> **BETTY**
> My little sister, don't worry. I will be your ears, and you will be my eyes.

Deana grasps Betty's hand, leads her to her bed, and tucks her in.

> **BETTY**
> Don't worry. If I can't see and you can't hear by tomorrow morning, then we will tell Mom and Dad. I love you, sister.

> **DEANA**
> I love you, too.

Blackout.

<u>Scene 6</u>

Lights rise. The parents are at the dining table.

> **ARLENE**
> Girls, get down here right now! It is getting late.

The two girls enter and approach the table. Deana holds Betty's arm, guiding her.

> **ARLENE**
> Deana, why are you leading Betty? She can walk on her own.

> **BETTY**
> Mom and Dad, I can't see anything, and Deana can't hear.

> **ARLENE**
> Don't play games with me. I have all I can do to put up with that man. (*She points to*

DENIAL, CONFRONTATION, OBSESSION AND RETURN

her husband.) I don't have time for your silly games.

WILLIAM
(*looking at Deana*)
Deana, why are you playing deaf?

Deana pulls out Betty's chair, then helps Betty sit down. Betty, frustrated, waves her hands.

BETTY
Dad, she can't hear you!

She knocks over a glass of milk.

ARLENE
Betty, stop being so clumsy!

Deana mops up the milk with her napkin, then helps Betty find her fork at the left of her plate.

ARLENE
I order you to stop playing games with me!

BETTY
(*crying*)
We are not playing games. I can't see, and Deana can't hear you. Please believe us.

WILLIAM
(*speaking softly*)
Girls, I want you to listen carefully and concentrate on what I am saying.

BETTY
Dad, I will listen, but Deana really can't hear you. I can hear you, but I can't see you.

ARLENE
Would you two stop—

WILLIAM
(*interrupting*)
For God's sake, be quiet and let me handle this! Betty, tell me, when did this happen?

BETTY
Last night.

WILLIAM
What about Deana?

BETTY
She was OK last night, but she went to your room and returned right away. I asked her what happened.

WILLIAM
What did she say?

BETTY
I can't hear.

ARLENE
Don't believe them. They are lying.

DENIAL, CONFRONTATION, OBSESSION AND RETURN

> **WILLIAM**
> Why would they lie about something like this?
>
> **ARLENE**
> Liars lie about everything.
>
> **WILLIAM**
> Please, girls, go back to your room. I need to talk to your mother.
>
> **BETTY**
> OK, Dad.

Betty gets up and reaches for Deana's arm. Slowly, the girls leave the dining room.

> **WILLIAM**
> Arlene, I watched Deana's body movements. I don't think she's faking. I also noticed when you spoke in an angry tone of voice, it did not seem to bother Deana, but it bothered Betty.
>
> **ARLENE**
> Let's observe them some more. Then we can see if they are telling the truth.

Blackout.

ACT II

Scene 1

Lights rise. William and Arlene are at the pediatrician's office.

PEDIATRICIAN
What brings you here today?

WILLIAM
This may sound incredible, but our oldest daughter, Betty, almost thirteen years old, says she is blind. Deana, eleven years old, says she cannot hear. At first, we thought they were faking it or playing a silly game with us.

PEDIATRICIAN
When did you first observe this?

WILLIAM
Yesterday. Since then, we have spent several hours watching them, and I have concluded they are not faking it. My wife disagrees with me.

PEDIATRICIAN
Where were they when this supposedly happened?

WILLIAM
I think in their room. We first noticed it when they came down for breakfast. At first, neither my wife nor I believed them.

DENIAL, CONFRONTATION, OBSESSION AND RETURN

PEDIATRICIAN
(*writing*)
Tell me more.

WILLIAM
Betty, the one who says she is blind, was walking very carefully and had to be assisted by her sister. At the breakfast table, my wife reprimanded Betty for spilling milk. Betty was annoyed by my wife's tone of voice, but Deana, who usually sulks when my wife corrects them, did not react this time.

PEDIATRICIAN
Thank you. Please go to the waiting room. My nurse will bring the girls for me to examine.

Blackout.

<u>Scene 2</u>

Lights rise. The pediatrician sits with William and Arlene.

PEDIATRICIAN
I examined Betty and Deana for about an hour, and I can't find any medical reason that substantiates their symptoms. However, Betty gave me the impression that she could not visually focus on anything. Deana was totally unresponsive when I gave her a test dealing with words and noises. It is highly unusual to have two siblings that develop sensory problems at the same time. I am

going to have Betty examined by an ophthalmologist and Deana by an audiologist.

Blackout.

<u>Scene 3</u>

Lights rise. Days later, William and Arlene are at the pediatrician's office.

          PEDIATRICIAN
Please, sit down. Well, first, I have good news. The specialist found absolutely no medical reason for Betty's blindness. The audiologist did not find any medical reason for Deana's deafness. Now the bad news. We three doctors discussed their symptoms. We agreed, without question, that their problems are psychological.

          ARLENE
Oh, Doctor, that is pure nonsense! Do you think I—

          WILLIAM
          (*interrupting*)
Arlene, tone it down, please. I am sorry, Doctor. What is our next move?

          PEDIATRICIAN
An examination of both girls by a psychiatrist who also specializes in neurology. You see, these are psychological

problems brought about by extreme unresolved conflicts causing their physical symptoms: psychological blindness and psychological deafness. In other words, high levels of stress that persist over time could account for the blindness and deafness that the girls are experiencing.

ARLENE
Never! My girls are not crazy.

PEDIATRICIAN
No one is saying the girls are crazy, but they definitely have some type of neurological problem. Before we can begin to treat them for their symptoms, diagnostic evaluations are necessary. We doctors need to know what we are treating.

ARLENE
(*reluctantly*)
Well, I—

WILLIAM
Doctor, continue, we will do what you tell us.

PEDIATRICIAN
I can recommend a psychiatrist.

Scene 4

Lights rise. Betty sits in the psychiatrist's office.

PSYCHIATRIST
How are you, Betty?

BETTY
Fine, Doctor, thank you.

PSYCHIATRIST
Betty, do you remember what you were doing just before you became blind?

BETTY
No. I just don't remember, Doctor.

PSYCHIATRIST
OK, tell me, Betty, have you been having any problems at school?

BETTY
No, Doctor, I love school. I am always happy at school, but when I… (*She drops her head.*) I don't want to talk about it.

PSYCHIATRIST
OK, then, let me ask you, Betty, are you happy at home?

BETTY
Well, sometimes…

PSYCHIATRIST
When you are not happy, why aren't you happy?

BETTY
Well, things are not always right.

PSYCHIATRIST
What things?

BETTY
I don't think Mom and Dad, especially Mom, really love Deana and me. Doctor, I don't want to talk anymore. May I go?

PSYCHIATRIST
Of course, Betty. Let my nurse take you to the waiting room.

Blackout.

Scene 5

Lights rise. Betty and the psychiatrist are at his office a few days later. The psychiatrist pats her hand.

PSYCHIATRIST
How are you today, Betty?

BETTY
(*timidly*)
I am fine, Doctor.

PSYCHIATRIST
I am so happy that you will talk to me again. Betty, tell me about your school and what you and your sister talk about.

BETTY
(*sad and withdrawn*)
I really like school, and I have lots of friends. I don't have any problems with my classmates. They all like me.

PSYCHIATRIST
Wonderful! Tell me about your teachers.

BETTY
I really like them, but my English teacher, I don't like her very much. She is very…

PSYCHIATRIST
She is very?

BETTY
She is very cranky and makes me nervous. She snaps at me and the other girls a lot.

PSYCHIATRIST
Do you have other female teachers?

BETTY
Yes, I have two now, and last semester, I had three. I liked all of them. They were not mean to me or the other students.

PSYCHIATRIST
Tell me about the English teacher you do not like.

DENIAL, CONFRONTATION, OBSESSION AND RETURN

> **BETTY**
> (*bowing her head*)
> She is just an old meanie. I don't learn very much from her.
>
> **PSYCHIATRIST**
> (*repeating*)
> I don't learn very much from her…
>
> **BETTY**
> I just sit there. I am scared of her. I don't even ask questions.
>
> **PSYCHIATRIST**
> Do the other female teachers make you feel the same way?
>
> **BETTY**
> No! They are all very nice.
>
> **PSYCHIATRIST**
> Betty, you have made it quite clear that you like your other teachers but not your English teacher. Tell me anything about the English teacher that you can think of.

Betty seems very nervous. She fidgets in her seat.

> **PSYCHIATRIST**
> Don't be afraid to tell me anything about that teacher. I am not going to tell anyone what you say. It is just between you and me. Betty, think of me as a loyal

friend who really likes you and respects you.

BETTY
One time, this teacher...

PSYCHIATRIST
(*repeating calmly*)
One time, this teacher...

BETTY
Doctor, I don't want to talk about her. She reminds me of...

PSYCHIATRIST
She reminds me of...

BETTY
(*agitated*)
I am sorry, Doctor. I just don't know.

Lights slowly dim.

Blackout.

<u>Scene 6</u>

Lights rise. Deana is at the psychiatrist's office. The psychiatrist walks in smiling with some painted cards in his hand.

PSYCHIATRIST
Good to see you, Deana. Sit down, please. (*pointing to a chair*) I am going to write in-

structions on the game we are going to play. We are going to read these cards together, and then I will tell you what to do.

The psychiatrist holds up a card and reads.

          PSYCHIATRIST
Tell me a story about this picture. An adult male, female, and a little girl.

          DEANA
It looks like a man, his wife, and their daughter.

Psychiatrist writes.

          PSYCHIATRIST
I have another card for us to see. Three faces, an adult male, an adult female, and a little girl. Tell me a story about what you see. Please make it very long. I like long stories.

          DEANA
They look angry, like Mom and Dad. The little girl looks sad. I bet she is crying.

          PSYCHIATRIST
Why is she crying?

          DEANA
I think she is afraid of that mean old Mommy and Daddy.

PSYCHIATRIST
(*writing on a card*)
Afraid of the mean old Mommy and Daddy?

DEANA
I bet Betty would also be afraid of those two people.

PSYCHIATRIST
How does Betty, your sister, feel about her female teachers?

DEANA
Betty likes them all, except for her English teacher. Betty told me one time that she is as mean as Mommy.

PSYCHIATRIST
Deana, you and I are going to read these cards together. I want you to complete this sentence. Take your time.

Psychiatrist looks at a card and reads.

PSYCHIATRIST
Number one: Sometimes I get scared…

DEANA
When Mom and Dad fight.

PSYCHIATRIST
Number two: At school, I like…

> DEANA
> When Betty, my friends, and I talk and laugh at recess.
>
> PSYCHIATRIST
> Number three: I don't like...
>
> DEANA
> When Betty cries or is very sad at home.
>
> PSYCHIATRIST
> Number four: Betty doesn't like...
>
> DEANA
> Her English teacher.
>
> PSYCHIATRIST
> Number five: The English teacher...
>
> DEANA
> Is very mean to Betty just like Mommy.
>
> PSYCHIATRIST
> Number six: At home, I...
>
> DEANA
> Am not very happy.
>
> PSYCHIATRIST
> Number seven: At home, Betty...

DEANA
Gets very upset when she hears Mom screaming at Dad.

PSYCHIATRIST
Number eight: At home, I…

DEANA
Used to get upset every time I heard Mom and Dad screaming at each other.

PSYCHIATRIST
Number nine: One time at home, I…

DEANA
Heard Dad screaming at Mommy that…they would put us…

She cries hysterically.

PSYCHIATRIST
Sometimes Betty and I wish…

DEANA
That Mommy were dead.

PSYCHIATRIST
(*writing on a card*)
Deana, why do you want Mommy dead?

DEANA
Well, even though I cannot hear Mommy, I still have to see her. If she were dead, I would not have to see her.

PSYCHIATRIST
Fine, fine. Let's stop for today. I will see you next week. You are doing well.

Blackout.

ACT III

<u>Scene 1</u>

Lights rise. William and Arlene are in the psychiatrist's office.

          PSYCHIATRIST
Good to see you. Please sit down. William and Arlene, as you know, I have spoken with the girls. I want to start therapy and see each one separately twice a week.

          WILLIAM
Yes, Doctor.

          PSYCHIATRIST
Before you go, I would like to ask you a few questions. You may think some of these questions are too personal and could make you feel uncomfortable, but they have to be asked. The problems with the girls are psychologically induced, and for me to get rid of their symptoms, blindness and deafness, I must get to the causes. Once I do that, therapy will be successful. Please understand, William and Arlene, I am not judging you. Again, I must remind you that I need to get all the information that I can as to what is going on in the girls' home environment.

          WILLIAM
Excuse me, Doctor, I am not sure where you are going with all this.

DENIAL, CONFRONTATION, OBSESSION AND RETURN

> **PSYCHIATRIST**
> William, there is no such thing as a perfect family.
>
> **WILLIAM**
> Doctor, Arlene and I have our differences. Probably, our girls have heard us quarrel now and then, but I can't remember saying something that would really upset them, let alone something traumatic.
>
> **PSYCHIATRIST**
> Arlene, I am asking you the same question.
>
> **ARLENE**
> Absolutely not! We are not dysfunctional people.
>
> **PSYCHIATRIST**
> OK, thank you. That is all for today.

Blackout.

Scene 2

Lights rise at the psychiatrist's office. The psychiatrist gently takes Betty's hand and guides her to a chair.

> **PSYCHIATRIST**
> Hello, Betty. Sit down, please. It is good to see you again. Are you comfortable?
>
> **BETTY**
> Yes, Doctor.

PSYCHIATRIST
I am going to try something a little bit different, if you don't mind. It is called hypnosis. Hypnosis is like going to sleep. There is nothing to fear. I want you to try to relax and sit in a comfortable position. If your body is too tense, it may not work well. Betty, before I begin, let me say this: I feel that something occurred when you were younger right up to just a few days ago that caused your blindness. That is why I need to use hypnosis. It may help you recall some earlier experiences that were quite unpleasant.

BETTY
OK, Doctor.

PSYCHIATRIST
(*in a reassuring and gentle tone*)
Just focus on the sound of my voice. Betty, your eyelids are beginning to get heavy. You are becoming drowsy. Your whole body wants to go to sleep.

Betty's head nods, then droops.

PSYCHIATRIST
Betty, did your mother ever get angry with you?

BETTY
Yes.

PSYCHIATRIST
Betty, did your mother and father get angry with each other in front of you?

BETTY
Yes.

PSYCHIATRIST
Betty, tell me how that made you feel.

Betty seems tense all of a sudden. She fidgets, then raises her head. Her eyes open.

BETTY
Hi, Doctor! I am awake.

PSYCHIATRIST
(*to himself*)
I am moving too fast. (*to Betty*) It is OK, Betty. Let's see if you can go back to sleep.

BETTY
OK, Doctor.

PSYCHIATRIST
Listen to the sound of my voice again. Betty, you are getting tired. Your eyelids are so heavy. Your eyelids are so heavy. You are going to sleep.

After a moment, Betty again relaxes, and her head droops.

> PSYCHIATRIST
> Betty, did you dislike one of your English teachers?

> BETTY
> Yes, her name was Mrs. Brown, and she was so mean to me and the other students. I hated her and feared her. I was afraid to ask her questions in class. She would snap at me the same way that...

Betty's body stiffens, and she wakes up again.

> BETTY
> (*nervously*)
> Doctor, I guess I am awake again.

> PSYCHIATRIST
> Don't worry. That is enough for today.

<u>Scene 3</u>

Lights rise. Two days later at the psychiatrist's office.

> PSYCHIATRIST
> Hello, Betty. It is good to see you. Sit down in this chair. (*He helps her sit down.*) I am going to hypnotize you like I did the other day. Relax and try to go to sleep.

BETTY
Yes, Doctor. I know how.

She is asleep within a few moments.

PSYCHIATRIST
Betty, tell me what your sister, Deana, and your parents talk about around the dinner table.

BETTY
Oh, just a lot of things. Mom and Dad do most of the talking.

PSYCHIATRIST
What do they talk about?

BETTY
(*irritated*)
I don't know.

PSYCHIATRIST
Are they angry when they talk?

BETTY
Yes, most of the time.

PSYCHIATRIST
Could you see anger in their faces? Did they point their fingers at each other?

Her body stiffens. She wakes up and seems more nervous than before.

> PSYCHIATRIST
> Betty, don't worry. We are making progress. Let's stop now. We will meet next week.

Blackout.

Scene 4

Lights rise on the psychiatrist's office. The psychiatrist guides Betty to a chair.

> PSYCHIATRIST
> Hello, Betty. It is good to see you. Please sit down in your comfortable chair. Today, we are going to try something called age regression. I am going to ask you questions about your life starting with the age of twelve and, perhaps, back to your childhood. Is that OK with you?

> BETTY
> Yes, Doctor.

> PSYCHIATRIST
> Let's begin. Just listen to the sound of my voice, and try to sleep like before.

After a moment, Betty's head droops.

> PSYCHIATRIST
> Betty, what bothered you the most about your English teacher and your parents when you were twelve years old?

DENIAL, CONFRONTATION, OBSESSION AND RETURN

BETTY
All three were cranky people, but Mom and the English teacher were the worst.

PSYCHIATRIST
Betty, tell me something that bothered you when you were ten years old.

BETTY
Mom and Dad were screaming at each other and pointing their fingers in each other's faces.

PSYCHIATRIST
Betty, tell me something that bothered you when you were eight years old.

BETTY
Oh, Doctor! I remember something that really upset me. Mom was screaming at Dad and saying bad things to him. My little sister burst into tears and put her hands over her ears. I just dropped my head and refused to look at them.

PSYCHIATRIST
Betty, can you remember anything bad that happened when you were six years old?

Betty mumbles in a childish tone.

PSYCHIATRIST
(*to himself*)
Good, she is in the somnambulistic phase.

Suddenly, Betty is horrified.

> BETTY
> (*screaming*)
> Mommy, don't stab Daddy! Please don't, Mommy!
>
> PSYCHIATRIST
> You're safe here, Betty. Tell me what happened.
>
> BETTY
> Dad tried to get a roll from the bread basket, and Mom took a fork and stabbed him.
>
> PSYCHIATRIST
> What did you do then?
>
> BETTY
> I got up and pulled the fork from Dad's bleeding hand and then threw the fork across the room.
>
> PSYCHIATRIST
> What did you say to your mother?
>
> BETTY
> (*trembling*)
> I hate you, Mother, and I am scared of you. I cannot even look at you. My eyes hurt when I see you.
>
> PSYCHIATRIST
> What did Deana do?

DENIAL, CONFRONTATION, OBSESSION AND RETURN

BETTY
I remember so well. She got up screaming and ran to her room with her little hands over her ears.

PSYCHIATRIST
Betty, when you were four years old, did anything happen that made you angry or sad?

BETTY
(*in a little child's voice*)
Yes, Doctor. I was cutting paper dolls, and Mom got mad at me for making a mess on the carpet.

PSYCHIATRIST
What did you do?

BETTY
I took my scissors and cut off the heads of the pictures of the women who looked like my mother.

PSYCHIATRIST
What did your mother do?

BETTY
(*crying like a child*)
She saw what I did, and she started slapping me on the top of my head. I just closed my eyes very tightly so I could not see her.

PSYCHIATRIST
Did Mom spank you when you were little?

BETTY
I don't know. All I can remember is that she was always screaming at Dad and saying that Deana and I were bad children.

PSYCHIATRIST
(*leaning toward her*)
Betty, when I count to three, you will wake up. One, two, three. Wake up, Betty.

BETTY
Hi, Doctor.

PSYCHIATRIST
Betty, can you see me at all?

BETTY
(*sadly*)
No, Doctor. I am still blind.

PSYCHIATRIST
Let's talk for a few minutes, and then I want you to continue to think about our conversation. Betty, you told me your mother stabbed your father when you were little. Think about that. Also, you told me your mother spanked you on top of the head when you were playing with paper dolls, and that made you feel sad. Betty, I realize you have learned to fear and hate your mother. Tell me, have

there been times when she showed love to
you?

BETTY
(*agitated*)
Yes…but I still hate her!

PSYCHIATRIST
You are doing fine, Betty. See you next week.
I want you to think about all those things
that you now remember.

Blackout.

Scene 5

Lights rise. One week later. Betty enters the doctor's office.

PSYCHIATRIST
Hello, Betty. Let me help you sit down in
your favorite chair.

BETTY
Thanks, Doctor.

PSYCHIATRIST
Betty, tell me something. Since I saw you
last, have you been thinking about our
conversation?

BETTY
I think I understand better now why I hate
Mom so much.

PSYCHIATRIST
Tell me.

BETTY
Believe it or not, now that I recall when Mom was out of control and violent, I feel better, but I still cannot see, and I still hate her.

PSYCHIATRIST
You can't see yet, because you can't stand the sight of her.

BETTY
I thought about what you first said.

PSYCHIATRIST
Tell me about it, Betty.

BETTY
I have thought about running away from home. I would be able to see again because I would not have to see my mother.

PSYCHIATRIST
Betty, let's stop for now. Let me say this before you leave. It is just a matter of time before you see again. After I see Deana, I am going to set up a meeting with your father and mother. I want you and Deana present. It is very important that you attend.

DENIAL, CONFRONTATION, OBSESSION AND RETURN

> **BETTY**
> Are you sure I will be able to see again?
>
> **PSYCHIATRIST**
> (*patting Betty gently on her shoulder and in a reassuring voice*)
> There is no doubt about it.
>
> **BETTY**
> Thanks, Doctor.

Blackout.

ACT IV

Scene 1

Lights rise at the psychiatrist's office. Deana enters.

                PSYCHIATRIST
            Hello, Deana. How are you?

Deana smiles. The psychiatrist points to a chair and shows Deana some cards.

                PSYCHIATRIST
        I have some cards with questions. I want you to read them several times and think about these questions. Then we'll try something called hypnosis. Follow these instructions.

He hands Deana another card.

                PSYCHIATRIST
        Deana, relax and gently stroke your arms. Also, see this shining object? I want you to focus on this shining object and, at the same time, think about the questions I had you read from the cards that you have on your lap.

He slightly moves the shining pocket watch back and forth, and he strokes his own arms. He acts as if he is going to sleep. In a few minutes, Deana leans forward with her eyes closed, and the cards slide out of her hands and onto the floor.

> **PSYCHIATRIST**
> (*to himself*)
> I believe she is in a somnambulistic trance.

Deana drops her head into her hands and screams hysterically.

> **DEANA**
> Mom, Mom, stop screaming! Dad, don't put us in an orphanage.

She sits up straight, looks at the doctor. There is fear in her voice.

> Doctor, Doctor, they haven't put us in an orphanage yet, maybe they won't.

Psychiatrist reaches for his pen to write something on a card for Deana to read.

> **DEANA**
> (*blurts out*)
> You don't need to write anything. I can hear you. (*She jumps out of her chair and hugs the doctor.*) I feel great.

> **PSYCHIATRIST**
> Wonderful, Deana, wonderful.

> **DEANA**
> Bye, Doctor.

> **PSYCHIATRIST**
> Wait, Deana, I want the whole family here next week.

DEANA
Do I really have to come? Now that I can hear, I don't think I am ready to hear my mother's voice.

PSYCHIATRIST
Deana, it is very important that you attend.

DEANA
OK, I will be here. I promise.

Blackout.

Scene 2

Lights rise. The entire family is sitting at the psychiatrist's office in a semicircle facing the audience.

PSYCHIATRIST
It is good that the five of us can sit together and say anything we want. Remember, not all families are always happy, but I believe that this family will have many happy years ahead. Arlene and William, do you have anything to say?

ARLENE
We are pleased that Deana can hear. When is Betty going to see?

PSYCHIATRIST
When she is ready. Deana, you can hear again. How does it feel?

DENIAL, CONFRONTATION, OBSESSION AND RETURN

> **DEANA**
> Fine, Doctor. You told me to always be honest with my feelings. (*looking at her mother and in a firm voice*) Mom, I am sorry to say this, but I am not sure that I am ready to hear your voice, and that worries me.

Arlene is irritated but silent.

> **PSYCHIATRIST**
> Betty, do you have anything to say to your parents?

> **BETTY**
> Yes, I do. Mom, I am not going to say that I am sorry. I am almost glad that I am still blind, but I wish I were deaf.

> **ARLENE**
> (*putting her hands over her eyes and sobbing hysterically*)
> Oh, girls! I am so sorry. I have been a mean and cranky person all my life. I have always blamed everyone but myself. (*still sobbing, looking at the girls*) Please forgive me. I need your love.

> **WILLIAM**
> Girls, we have made mistakes that have caused you turmoil. (*sadly*) Please forgive us. I will never do anything to harm you or your mother. We love you so much.

BETTY
Deana, please lead me to Dad.

Deana does. Betty reaches out to touch her dad's face.

BETTY
Well... (*Her voice changes, and she screams with joy.*) Mom, Dad, I can see again! (*She hugs her dad.*) Daddy, I know you will not strangle Mom, and I know you love me. (*She turns to her mother.*) Mom, I forgive you, and I love you. It will be nice to have meals in the dining room and see you both happy.

DEANA
(*putting her hand on her mother's shoulder*)
Mom, I am glad I can hear your voice. We will talk at the dinner table. It will be fun.

PSYCHIATRIST
It is a joy for me to see you loving each other, but I need to say something.
You have come a long way, but I have observed similar situations where there can be a relapse by one of you or all of you. In other words, William and Arlene, you may unconsciously behave the way you did before, and fall into the trap of denial. Betty and Deana, you both have experienced a conversion hysterical reaction. All that means is your stress was transformed, that is, converted into a physical symptom, which gave you

some relief from stress in the short run, but complicated and created more problems for you. So girls, if you sense that your deafness or blindness is reappearing, then please contact me. Also, Arlene and William, I would like for you to do the same. In fact, all of you may benefit from additional sessions of family counseling. You see, the problem is in the family, not just in you as individuals.

Blackout.

Scene 3

Lights rise. A few months later. The family is seated at the dining-room table, lit in a soft spotlight. William and Arlene pantomime an argument, their faces full of rage. Arlene lifts up her side of the table, and everything falls off: food, dishes, silverware, glasses.

Blackout.

Scene 4

Dim lights outside a door to the psychiatrist's office. Deana leads Betty by the hand.

DEANA
Betty, we are almost there. When the doctor sees us, he will know why we are back.

Lights slowly fade.

A Tale of Three Selfies

CHARACTERS

PAIGE, a paranoid woman in her early twenties
OLGA, an obsessive-compulsive woman in her early twenties
NATALIE, a narcissistic woman in her early twenties
KAREN, a graduate student in her late twenties
WAITRESS, a woman in her forties
WAITER #1, a man in his early thirties
WAITER #2, a man in his twenties
MAN AT RESTAURANT
WOMAN AT RESTAURANT

LOCATION

Minneapolis, Minnesota

TIME

Present day

ACT I

Scene 1

Lights rise on a college campus hallway. Paige, Olga, and Natalie look at a bulletin board. Paige points at one of the fliers.

>PAIGE
>
>Hey, girls! Look at this! Three bedrooms, one bath, and a garage close to campus. Lease for two semesters. Partially furnished. (*She takes a picture of the flier with her cell phone.*)
>
>OLGA
>
>If I am going to share the kitchen, it has to be neat.
>
>NATALIE
>
>Only one bathroom?
>
>PAIGE
>
>Oh, we can do it. Let's see if we can all live together.
>
>OLGA
>
>We'll each have our own room. It'll be less expensive than living by ourselves.

Blackout.

Scene 2

Lights rise, showing the kitchen and living room of the apartment. Olga and Natalie check out the place. A daybed, a desk, and a lamp are in a corner of the living room.

> OLGA
> Look! If you don't mind another roommate, we can rent out that corner of the living room to a poor graduate student.
>
> NATALIE
> And the rent will be cheaper. Let's go and see the bulletin board. Maybe someone is looking.

Blackout.

Scene 3

Lights rise. A week later at the apartment. Karen is sitting at the desk.

> KAREN
> I am very happy here. You girls are lovely.
>
> OLGA
> Do you ever go out?
>
> KAREN
> I don't have the money.
>
> NATALIE
> What is the topic of your thesis?

DENIAL, CONFRONTATION, OBSESSION AND RETURN

          KAREN
Well, my masters is in clinical psychology. My advisor suggested I do a field study.

          NATALIE
What is that?

          KAREN
It is a collection of information based on observation by living with the subjects. My thesis advisor suggested that I go to the jungle in Brazil, but I don't have the money to go, so I have to do something else. I have to stay here and find my subjects. I will do fine.

Scene 4

Lights rise. Natalie and Paige are sitting in the living room. Karen lies on the daybed. Olga is in the kitchen.

          OLGA
Look at this mess! Dishes left in the sink from last night. The tub has a ring! Who took a bath last night and did not clean the tub? Tell me, people!

          NATALIE
Who are you? Our mother?

          KAREN
         (waking up and rubbing her eyes)
I might as well get up and write.

OLGA
Right now, we are going to set some rules to follow.

PAIGE
Who will set the rules, you?

OLGA
I know how to do it! I will print and post them in the kitchen and in your bedrooms.

PAIGE
Wait a minute. Nobody is allowed to enter my bedroom. My room will always be locked.

OLGA
I understand. Nobody is allowed to enter my bedroom, either. You people might disturb the perfect order of my things.

NATALIE
Nobody goes into my room. You might disturb all my mirrors and pictures. Speaking of which... (*She takes a selfie.*)

OLGA
(*writing*)
Very good. Rule number one: Nobody is allowed to enter each other's bedrooms.

PAIGE
What if there is an emergency?

DENIAL, CONFRONTATION, OBSESSION AND RETURN

> **OLGA**
> Take off your shoes before you enter my room! I don't like dirt from the soles of your shoes on my floor.

Blackout.

<u>Scene 5</u>

Lights rise. Paige and Olga are pounding on the bathroom door.

> **PAIGE**
> Hurry up! We have to get ready. You have been in there for over an hour. We have a class at nine o'clock.

> **OLGA**
> If you don't get out right now, I'll take the door off.

Natalie flings open the door, her hair and makeup perfectly done.

> **NATALIE**
> Girls, you can see I left everything in order: No hair in the vanity, and no ring in the tub.

> **PAIGE**
> Just let us in.

Blackout.

Scene 6

Lights rise. Natalie and Paige are sitting in the living room, and Karen is writing in her corner.

> NATALIE
> Paige, how was your exam?

> PAIGE
> Well, today the professor returned our exams. He said only three people did well on their essays, though it should've only been me. They stole my ideas! They peeked at my answers when the professor wasn't looking. They don't like me. They have been insanely jealous of me since high school. Well, maybe they did not look during the exam, but during the break, they looked at my notes and got my ideas. To me, that is cheating. Yes, cheating!

> NATALIE
> Paige, I understand. Let me tell you what happened today in my class. The professor asked a complicated question. Of course, I knew the answer, but I wanted to give other people a chance. The professor told the students, "Excellent." As I was leaving the classroom, I felt good because I knew my answer could have been a thousand times better. A student waited for me, her eyes were full of pride, so I told her, "Your ideas were absurd. The professor just wanted you to feel good.

DENIAL, CONFRONTATION, OBSESSION AND RETURN

To me, your responses were shallow and stupid." Would you believe what she said to me? "Natalie, who do you think you are? Miss Superiority?" I answered, "I did not say that, you did."

Blackout.

Scene 7

Lights rise. Olga is cleaning in the kitchen. Natalie and Paige are in the living room. Karen is at the desk.

OLGA
Who on earth left this mess?

PAIGE
(*entering the kitchen*)
I am sorry. I was preparing something, and my phone rang in the bedroom. Stop making a big deal out of it.

OLGA
Excuses, excuses. I am sick of excuses. Everything should be put in order immediately. Do your hear me?

PAIGE
OK, Miss Perfect. I'll clean right now. You can inspect it later with your white gloves.

Olga leaves offstage, then screams.

> OLGA'S VOICE
> Somebody! Come to my room and help me!

Natalie jumps up and runs offstage.

> NATALIE'S VOICE
> What is it?

> OLGA'S VOICE
> Take off your shoes!

> NATALIE'S VOICE
> OK, OK! What's wrong, Olga?

> OLGA'S VOICE
> Look at that line of dirt in the carpet! I can't stand dirt. I have been scrubbing and can't remove it.

> NATALIE'S VOICE
> Let me see. Let's get some light in here.

The sound of blinds opening offstage.

> OLGA'S VOICE
> It's gone!

> NATALIE'S VOICE
> Oh, for goodness' sake! It was just the sunlight shining through the blinds.

> OLGA'S VOICE
> Oh! Thanks.

DENIAL, CONFRONTATION, OBSESSION AND RETURN

Karen continues to write.

Blackout.

Scene 8

Lights rise. Natalie is taking a selfie in the living room while Karen writes. Olga enters.

> OLGA
> How was the shopping?

> NATALIE
> I just went to walk, but Paige saw a dress she liked.

> OLGA
> Did she buy it?

> NATALIE
> She asked the price, but then she argued that it was supposed to be twenty percent off. She asked to see the manager. He explained to her the twenty percent off was for the weekend only, and today was Monday. I was so embarrassed that I left the store. When she came out, she told me the manager put her down and that he was a jerk. I thought the manager was polite, but she said he was mean and that she could not make him change his mind.

Blackout.

Scene 9

Lights rise. Paige, Olga, Natalie, and Karen are sitting at the apartment.

> **OLGA**
> It's Friday. Let's go out to that new Italian restaurant.
>
> **NATALIE**
> Let's go. We need to get away from the books. Karen, come with us. You never go out. All you do is write.
>
> **KAREN**
> Yes, it would be good to get out of the apartment, and I did get paid today.

Scene 10

Lights rise at La Dolce Vita restaurant. Paige, Olga, Natalie, and Karen sit at a table.

> **WAITRESS**
> (*smiling*)
> Welcome to La Dolce Vita.
>
> **OLGA**
> The letter *c* in Italian is pronounced as *ch* before *e*. Listen to my pronunciation: "La Dolce Vita." They did not train you well.

DENIAL, CONFRONTATION, OBSESSION AND RETURN

WAITRESS
(*annoyed*)
Would you like to order now?

PAIGE
Please, for me, lasagna.

NATALIE
Please, lasagna for me, too.

KAREN
Per favore. Risotta di Gambero e Asparagi.

OLGA
(*surprised*)
Karen, do you speak Italian?

KAREN
Yes. I lived in Florence, Italy for a year.

WAITRESS
(*looking at Olga*)
Would you like to order now?

OLGA
Fettucine Alfredo, but before I decide for sure, tell me, do you really use grated Romano cheese and real butter? Do you know the total number of carbohydrates and saturated fat per serving?

> **WAITRESS**
> (*confused and mildly irritated*)
> Sorry, miss.

She leaves the table. A waiter arrives, smiling.

> **WAITER #1**
> *Buonasera.*

> **OLGA**
> I hope you are more efficient than the other waitress. I need to know the carbohydrates of the fettucine Alfredo.

> **WAITER #1**
> (*speaking quickly*)
> Forty-two grams of carbohydrates, five hundred and nine calories, fourteen grams of fat, one hundred sixty-seven milligrams of cholesterol, and seven hundred twenty-four milligrams of sodium.

> **OLGA**
> (*surprised*)
> How do you know all that?

> **WAITER #1**
> I am a nutritionist. Anything else?

Blackout.

DENIAL, CONFRONTATION, OBSESSION AND RETURN

Scene 11

Lights rise. Karen is writing in her corner. Natalie, Paige, and Olga are sitting in the living room.

        PAIGE
        (*annoyed, holding a newspaper*)
It kills me when I read about politics.

        NATALIE
        (*taking a selfie*)
Then don't read about it.

        PAIGE
I want to be well informed, so when I speak with other people, I have already gathered considerable information. If you two don't agree with me, I don't care. (*raising her voice*) Do you hear me? I don't care what you think. I am always right!

        OLGA
Slow down, Paige. We are your friends.

        PAIGE
When I was speaking, you two looked at me as if I were nothing. Are you going to persecute me for my politics?

        NATALIE
Come on, Paige. We respect each other. The way you are passionate about your ideas,

we are equally passionate about ours. Let's smile! (*She takes a selfie.*)

                PAIGE

You two are against everything I say, and I am sick of it. You have one intention, and it is to put me down. Maybe my ideas are more important and valid than yours.

Paige exits. The lights dim, then rise to show the passage of time. Paige is in the kitchen. Natalie flips through a magazine. Karen writes at the desk. Olga enters the kitchen.

                PAIGE

I am preparing some coffee. Would you like some?

                OLGA

Of course, thanks.

Olga's cell phone rings in her pocket.

                OLGA

Excuse me. (*She answers her phone.*) Yes, Susan. I agree with you. (*pause*) That is a great idea. (*pause*) Yes, at the student union. (*pause*) Paige and Natalie are fine. (*pause*) We are having coffee. (*pause*) See you tomorrow.

She ends the call, returns the phone to her pocket.

> OLGA
> That was Susan asking about a project for our sociology class. I like Susan. She is nice. Oh, she said to tell you hello.
>
> PAIGE
> I don't think I like Susan. She is rude, insensitive, and...I just don't trust her.
>
> OLGA
> She sounded very sincere when she asked about you two.
>
> NATALIE
> I like her. She is nice.
>
> PAIGE
> (*agitated and pacing the floor*)
> Can't you see what is going on here? She knows that you and Natalie like me, so she is going to say good things about me, but when you two are not around and I am in her presence, she is cruel, insensitive, and enjoys hurting my feelings.

Olga and Natalie look at each other and seem disappointed.

Blackout.

Scene 12

Lights rise. Natalie is in the kitchen. Karen writes at the desk. Paige rushes in from offstage, screaming.

> PAIGE
> Somebody has been in my room!

> NATALIE
> You sound like one of the Three Bears: "Somebody has been lying in my bed."

> PAIGE
> Stop it! I'm serious about this.

Olga enters.

> OLGA
> Paige, do you really think we went into your room and got into your computer and things?

> PAIGE
> Well, I don't know. Listen, Olga, that reminds me. Susan was over here the other day studying with you here in the kitchen. Tell me, do you remember? Look at me!

> OLGA
> Ask me whatever you want, but don't be so cranky. Yes, Susan and I had a test the next day.

DENIAL, CONFRONTATION, OBSESSION AND RETURN

PAIGE
When I was leaving the apartment, I did not go to the kitchen because I can't stand Susan. Please tell me the truth. When I was gone, did Susan leave the kitchen for any reason?

OLGA
Yes, a couple of times. She went to the bathroom, and I went to my bedroom to answer my cell phone.

PAIGE
That damn Susan, I knew it! I bet that damn girl was in my room snooping around. I just know it was Susan.

OLGA
Slow down, Paige. Tell me, why would you think that about my friend?

PAIGE
(*speaking in a low voice and looking around*)
Do you remember a couple of months ago when Susan was here and you two were watching TV?

OLGA
Sure, I remember.

PAIGE
I came in and sat down. I told you about my ex-boyfriend, nothing really that personal.

Just the reasons why I broke off our relationship, and why I lost respect for him. Do you remember, Olga?

OLGA
Yes, yes, I do. I also remember that you complained that he continued to send you e-mails.

PAIGE
Yes. Some of them were statements he made about our relationship. Remember, I told you I was not going to discuss anything with you girls.

OLGA
(*annoyed*)
Yes, yes.

PAIGE
That Susan had the gall to ask me questions about him! Questions I did not want to talk about.

NATALIE
Stop it, Paige. Breathe deeply! Relax! One, two, three.

PAIGE
Let me express myself. You breathe deeply. Besides my lack of trust for her, I also question her values. Yes, she went to my room and looked through some of my e-mails.

NATALIE
Does she know your password?

PAIGE
With her evil mind, I bet she guessed it.
I know she is talking to all her girlfriends
about me and making me look like a fool.
Her intentions toward me are evil.

Blackout.

Scene 13

Lights rise. Olga and Karen are in the kitchen.

OLGA
Karen, why do you never go out?

KAREN
I don't have money. My graduate assistant-
ship covers my rent and food. That is all.

OLGA
Also, why are you always writing? Day and
night, that is all you do.

KAREN
Writing takes so much time!

Blackout.

ACT II

Scene 1

Lights rise. The three girls are in the kitchen, and Karen is listening to their conversation.

          PAIGE
I am thinking of dropping my sociology class.

          OLGA
          (*surprised*)
What's wrong? You said you got A's on all your tests.

          PAIGE
Yes, but every time I speak up, the professor puts me down, or other students attack my views in such a negative and cruel way! Let me tell you what happened today. On the way out of class, several students looked at me and started whispering. I could not hear what they were saying, but I know, I just know they were talking about me. I am sick and tired of the way people in that class treat me.

          NATALIE
You're not the only one. You would be surprised about the negative treatment I get from others because of my brains and beauty. (*She takes a selfie.*)

DENIAL, CONFRONTATION, OBSESSION AND RETURN

Olga opens the refrigerator, then yells.

> **OLGA**
> Who made this mess? The caps are off the sauces. Food is dripping out of the containers. The cheese is not where it is supposed to be. I hate messy things. I can't stand a lack of order and a messy refrigerator. You two, I beg you to clean up your own messes. I cannot live in a pigsty.

Dim light on Karen as she writes and observes from her corner.

Blackout.

Scene 2

Lights rise. The three girls are relaxing in the living room while Karen writes.

> **OLGA**
> Today I went to the student union for the last time.

> **PAIGE**
> You enjoy going there. Why the change?

> **OLGA**
> The tables are sticky and messy. No one busses the trays.

> **PAIGE**
> Well, I don't want to go to school anymore.

I love learning, but the way I am treated is horrible. People laugh at me. I know what they are saying is offensive. I just feel like going over to them and scratching out their eyes.

NATALIE
Girls, what really bugs me is when others disapprove of me or criticize me simply because I am beautiful and intelligent. (*She takes a selfie.*) As you have heard me say before, I get cruel treatment all the time, even in my classes. When I was attending a meeting of the Student Body Governing Board, I got so tired of the female board members. They were so jealous of my good looks that I actually went to the bathroom and scrubbed all the makeup off of my face. I even felt that I should not express my views in any matter relating to the governing board. They were all so jealous of my intelligence and well-thought-out ideas. Even the guys seem to resent me. I got so fed up, I quit my position. Tell me girls, what am I supposed to do? Find a way to lower my IQ and run around with dirty hair and no makeup? (*She takes another selfie.*)

OLGA
(*looking at Karen's corner*)
Karen, by the way, we want to take you out for your birthday. Please accept our invitation.

> KAREN
> Thank you, girls. I would love it.

Blackout.

Scene 3

Lights rise at a crowded restaurant. The four are seated at a table. Olga snaps her fingers for attention.

> OLGA
> Where are our drinks? Service, please! Right now!

Waiter #2 comes over with a tray of drinks. He places them around the table. He leaves.

> OLGA
> OK, girls, let's sing. "Happy birthday to Karen."

The three start to join in, but Paige gets excited and spills half of her drink on Olga's dress.

> OLGA
> For God's sake, be careful! Make a mess on your own dress, not mine.

> PAIGE
> I am so sorry, but please don't persecute me. I am getting enough of that at school.

> OLGA
> OK, but you know I don't like messes.

Natalie stands.

> NATALIE
> Excuse me, girls. Gotta freshen up.

Natalie walks past a man and a woman seated at a table.

> MAN AT RESTAURANT
> Boy, look at that beauty.

> WOMAN AT RESTAURANT
> Her dress is too tight and her makeup is terrible.

Natalie turns around, sits back at her friends' table.

> NATALIE
> Did you hear that?

> OLGA
> Yes, we heard. You know you are pretty and a great dresser.

Natalie tosses back her drink quickly and signals Waiter #2 for another one.

> NATALIE
> I meant to tell you. I am entering a beauty contest, and I just know I will win. (*She takes a selfie.*)

PAIGE
Good idea.

OLGA
We are sure you will win.

Blackout.

Scene 4

Lights rise in the living room. Natalie primps in front of a mirror, smoothing her hair and eyebrows, then puckering her lips as if she were going to kiss herself. Karen writes. Paige reads.

NATALIE
Karen, do you think I am beautiful?

KAREN
You are very attractive and I know something about beauty. I did some modeling in high school.

Olga enters.

OLGA
Did you make a mess in the bathroom?

NATALIE
No, I just fixed my hair.

OLGA
Keep the bathroom as beautiful as you are, OK?

NATALIE
I will try, Olga. Paige, I meant to ask you about the guy you met the other day?

PAIGE
He is nice but too sensitive for me. You know me; sometimes I come on pretty strong, but he always seems to personalize so many things that I say. He was sweet, not as domineering and not as envious as most of the jerks that I have dated. You know, girls, most guys seem to enjoy persecuting me just because I have a strong personality. Did I tell you about the last time I saw him? We were talking and two other jerks who are in the same class began talking to me. At first, the conversation seemed pleasant, but I began to passionately express my views on an issue that the professor had raised in class. Before you know it, both of these jerks jumped all over me and put me down. (*speaking quickly*) My friend and I went into the classroom, and the two jerks told the people around them in a loud voice, "Be careful what you say to her, or she will jump all over you." Then the other guy said, "Stop persecuting me." Ha, ha. Then one said, "She is paranoid as hell." And do you know, Natalie and Olga, what is so ridiculous is that they are the paranoid ones.

Natalie and Olga nod in agreement.

OLGA
Karen, what do you think of all this?

KAREN
This is what happens with people who have a history of problems. They get aggressive and engage in denial. All you are doing when you continue to indulge in denial is postpone a solution to your problems.

OLGA
For God's sake, Karen, give us a break. You shrinks are all alike. Every time you see someone, you think they need help. Did you ever stop to think that maybe you psychologists need us more than we need you?

KAREN
Paige asked for my opinion.

OLGA
OK, Karen, I have nervous habits; I repeat things, and I am a stickler for order. But instead of being problems, these characteristics are avenues that will help me become successful in the real world. Quite frankly, Karen, maybe you have a problem. You sit up all night writing notes. How does that make you different from us?

KAREN
Well, Olga, for one thing, I don't go to my bedroom and cry and then come out and act irritably toward Paige and Natalie. When I first moved here, I did not see your behavior as that extreme, but now I do. Unless you get some help, you are going to go off the deep end and lose the control you are constantly seeking.

Before Olga can respond to Karen's assessment, Natalie blurts out.

NATALIE
Do you really think you are more intelligent than us? I have had lots of conversations with my girlfriends, and I have helped them a lot. They have told me so. I am the first to admit that the three of us have problems, but who doesn't? I also agree with Olga that your lifestyle is at least partly neurotic, but you are doing OK with it, so why can't Olga? I think Olga is doing quite well in her life. Karen, you may have studied psychology, but I think I know more about Olga and Paige and human behavior than you do. In fact, in my classes, all the students and my professors say I am quite bright and insightful. So, what do you think about that?

KAREN
Natalie, I originally thought that your inflated self-image, along with your self-confidence, was your greatest strength. Now,

DENIAL, CONFRONTATION, OBSESSION AND RETURN

however, after being around you for almost two semesters and listening to your conversations with Olga and Paige, I am beginning to think that those characteristics are your greatest weaknesses.

NATALIE
What on earth are you talking about?

KAREN
(*smiling in a teasing manner*)
Well, Natalie, I am talking about you, your favorite topic. Your self-love and adulation is out of control. I sense you are a very lonely person. You want to love others for who they are, but you can't because you won't let them in. Natalie, you don't have room for them. You are too busy loving yourself.

NATALIE
Well, I listen to my friends.

KAREN
Yes, yes, you do, as long as they are talking in such a way that it feeds your self-image. Your love is unilateral, yes, a one-way street. And you know what, Natalie? That is not mature love. It is narcissistic love.

NATALIE
Karen, are you calling me narcissistic?

KAREN
(*smiling*)
You raised the question.

NATALIE
Oh, for God's sake, spare me from this twenty-five-cent shrink. I have heard enough of this. Paige, what do you think of all this psychobabble? Olga and I think it is just pure nonsense.

PAIGE
I think it is more than pure nonsense. Personally, I think Karen is persecuting me. I don't think she likes me at all. Whenever I talk to her, she is cold and unfriendly. She treats me as if I don't even exist.

Paige stands up, glares at Karen, and starts yelling.

PAIGE
I am sick of you! Sick of you! The other night when you were watching TV with Olga and Natalie, I offered to bring you a cup of coffee, and you replied with coldness and indifference. "I can get it myself, thanks." Then, later, I could hear your part of the conversation clearly, and it was all about me. I am convinced, by your tone of voice, that you, Karen, hate me. You hate me! And I know you are trying to sour Olga on me. Olga does pick on me about not cleaning

the refrigerator, and I think she takes it too far, but Olga does not turn against me. You, Karen, certainly have.

KAREN
When I moved into this apartment, I told you that some people see me as cold, but it does not seem to bother them. They just accept me as I am, but you, Paige, you take things too personally, and read into things that are not my true thoughts and feelings about you. Paige, you often behave defensively with such aggressive feelings toward me. At first, I thought, well, just a personality conflict. But now I really do believe you have a serious problem in that you think practically everyone is persecuting you and wants to do you harm.

PAIGE
Well, everyone feels that way to a degree.

KAREN
Yes, Paige. Yes, you are right about "everyone," but your feelings of persecution and your constant personalization sets you apart from most other people. You have even admitted that it is getting more difficult to get along with others. These feelings of persecution and suspicion of others are going to destroy you if you don't do something about them.

Karen stands up.

> **KAREN**
> OK, girls, I think we have had enough for tonight, but I want you to know that I sincerely care about you, and I would like to help you. Maybe we can talk one-on-one.

Blackout.

ACT III

<u>Scene 1</u>

Lights rise. Karen and Olga are sitting in Karen's corner.

              KAREN
I am glad you are here. I was getting concerned when I saw you depressed, irritable, and sleeping so much during the day.

              OLGA
You are right, Karen. I have been playing this through my mind.

              KAREN
Yes, your obsessive-compulsive rituals are also getting out of control. That concerns me.

              OLGA
              (*upset*)
Please don't call them obsessive-compulsive rituals. They are just nervous habits.

              KAREN
OK, OK. Your nervous habits are no longer working for you.

              OLGA
What do you mean my nervous habits are not working for me?

KAREN
You are having trouble functioning in your daily life. Recognize it, Olga! This is a sign you are getting close to a full-blown neurosis.

OLGA
You mean a nervous breakdown?

KAREN
Yes, in other words, your everyday life functions are being interfered with.

OLGA
(*crying*)
You are right, Karen, you are right.

KAREN
I saw you checking the refrigerator and faucets over and over again. Of course, this kind of behavior wears you down.

OLGA
I am so tired in the morning that I have to sleep during the day.

KAREN
Of course, you have to compensate for it.

OLGA
I have also missed several classes.

KAREN
You even told your girlfriends that two of your professors asked you several times if you were OK because you appeared so tired, and your grades—

OLGA
(*interrupting*)
Yes, my grades are slipping.

KAREN
Paige and Natalie have told me that you are always nervous and can't relax, and it is getting worse.

OLGA
Why are they talking about me? They have their own problems too. You know this.

KAREN
Let me finish, Olga. They are saying you are no fun to be around.

OLGA
(*irate*)
I wish they would tell me that to my face rather than talking behind my back.

KAREN
Tell me how you feel about all of this.

OLGA
Well, I agree with some of the things you have said, but I still think I can work through my problems on my own. (*Suddenly, she bursts into tears and drops her head.*) I just don't know what to do about all of this.

KAREN
(*hugging Olga*)
I will help you, and we will work this out together.

OLGA
Please, Karen, tell me why do I have such an obsession for order and the need to control everything?

KAREN
How did it make you feel when you first started engaging in this compulsive behavior?

OLGA
(*speaking in a low voice*)
Better. I could even relax and concentrate better.

KAREN
Now this obsession for control and order and the resulting compulsive behavior is not only self-defeating, but it could get self-destructive.

DENIAL, CONFRONTATION, OBSESSION AND RETURN

OLGA
(*indignant*)
Karen, stop! I don't feel self-destructive.

KAREN
No, not yet, because you are taking your frustration and aggression out on others.

OLGA
I don't take my frustration out on others!

KAREN
Let me finish! Your problems and behavior are not entirely different from a casual drinker who becomes an alcoholic.

OLGA
I don't understand.

KAREN
When an alcoholic first starts drinking to relieve himself from stress, it works. But after a while, he has to drink more and more to get relief from his stress and anxiety. Then, of course, his drinking becomes so harmful, he has to get some help for the problem.

OLGA
Why have I developed such self-defeating patterns of behavior?

KAREN
You are psychologically desperate, so you engage in ego-defensive behavior in an effort to cope.

OLGA
Drinking to cope?

KAREN
Of course not. I am comparing your behavior to that of the alcoholic in order for you to get a better understanding of yourself. But you must understand, such behavior is just a short-term solution.

OLGA
Like a cover-up?

KAREN
Yes, an ego-defensive maneuver that your mind designs to keep something repressed in your unconscious.

OLGA
Why do I do that?

KAREN
Because we tend to take the easy way out, and unfortunately, the easy way out does not work in the long run.

OLGA
(*sobbing*)
Please, Karen, tell me. What can I do?

> KAREN
> We must begin by attempting to get to the root of your symptoms: obsession with order, need for control, et cetera. Why don't we meet twice a week? I am certain that I can help you.
>
> OLGA
> Thank you, Karen. Thank you.

Blackout.

Scene 2

Lights rise. Karen and Natalie are sitting in Karen's corner.

> KAREN
> Natalie, I am glad that you are willing to talk with me.
>
> NATALIE
> Quite frankly, Karen, I think this therapy is all nonsense. I am perfectly capable of working out my own problems. I can solve problems or do anything. Yes, Karen, anything. When I set my mind to something, I do it better than anyone else.
>
> KAREN
> Well, Natalie, based on what you just said, why are you here?

NATALIE
(*laughing*)
I think it will be fun. Olga enjoyed talking to you, and she said I would, too. Also, Karen, I think you are cool.

KAREN
Natalie, I have listened, sometimes even eavesdropped, on your conversations with Olga and Paige.

NATALIE
Eavesdropped? What kind of person are you?

KAREN
Slow down, Natalie. I live in this apartment in a little corner where I can see the kitchen, the living room, and the three doors to your bedrooms. Sometimes I could not help but listen to your conversations with Olga and Paige. I can see that you have a problem relating to others and keeping friends for a long time.

NATALIE
I have lots of friends.

KAREN
I also heard you say that you want to fall in love.

NATALIE
Yes, what is wrong with that?

KAREN
Nothing, but you keep saying that men don't meet your standards, and they are all "complete jerks."

NATALIE
Again, what is wrong with that?

KAREN
Well, with that attitude, you are never going to find the right guy. I also remember you saying to the other girls that the guy has to be perfect and constantly tell you how beautiful and intelligent you are.

NATALIE
(*laughing*)
Oh, they are exaggerating. I have high standards and high expectations for men, but also for people in general. That is just the way I am. Karen, I am not going to waste my time with losers and inferior people.

KAREN
Natalie, don't you think that you are taking it too far?

NATALIE
No, absolutely not!

KAREN
Listen very carefully, Natalie. I have known women like that, and frequently they end up lonely old women who develop drinking problems.

NATALIE
I will find the love of my life. Do you hear me, Karen?

KAREN
Yes, Natalie, I hear you. I want you to think about something. When you say, "I will find the love of my life," maybe you should examine what the "I" really means. It could be part of your problem when relating to men and friends in general.

NATALIE
(*laughing*)
OK, Miss Shrink, I will think about it.

KAREN
Also, Natalie, please reflect on another thing that I really do believe fits you.

NATALIE
Oh! Another thing?

KAREN
Yes. Let us refer to love first and friendships later. Natalie, love has to be a two-way street. Problems frequently arise when one party

in the relationship spends too much time indulging in self-love.

NATALIE
Me? Too much self-love?

KAREN
Yes, self-love. They also call it narcissism, and that type of person does not have enough love left over for the other party.

NATALIE
(*in a very stern voice*)
Are you implying, Miss Psychology, that I am just hung up on myself?

KAREN
(*in a soft voice*)
Just think about it, Natalie.

Natalie gets up and leaves Karen's corner.

KAREN
Will I see you again?

NATALIE
(*sarcastically*)
I will think about it.

She goes to her room and slams the door shut.

Blackout.

Scene 3

Lights rise. Paige sits in Karen's corner.

          KAREN
Hello, Paige! Welcome to my little corner. How are you today?

          PAIGE
I am fine.

          KAREN
Well, good! I thought it would be a good idea for the two of us to sit down and talk about things.

          PAIGE
What things?

          KAREN
Oh, just things in general like how your life is going. As you know, I have been talking to Olga and Natalie.

          PAIGE
Well, OK, but I don't want to hear how I need to change my ways, et cetera, and I don't like it when people constantly pick on me and put me down.

          KAREN
Why do you think people don't like you and put you down?

DENIAL, CONFRONTATION, OBSESSION AND RETURN

PAIGE
They don't appreciate the things in life that I think are important.

KAREN
What things? Tell me about them.

PAIGE
Well, since they don't appreciate what I appreciate, people are against me. Karen, I know people can be mean and cruel. Some wish me ill will and have evil, yes, evil, intentions toward me. One of Olga's friends, Susan, is like that. She is insensitive to me, and I just know that she disapproves of me. I suspect she is out to get me.

KAREN
Paige, do you think that your roommates are against you?

PAIGE
Well, I don't know. (*raising her voice*) But they are always telling me that I am overly sensitive and at times paranoid.

Paige gets up and paces the floor.

PAIGE
That damn Susan! I just know that when she was visiting Olga the other day, she went into my room, my sanctuary. She looked at my e-mails. I know she did! Karen, there were

many personal letters from my boyfriend.
I know she is going to talk about them and
even manufacture stories that I am a promiscuous woman. Susan is evil, and she wants
others to think that I am evil, too!

KAREN
I heard you in the kitchen when you were
having coffee with Olga and Natalie. You
were complaining about one of your classes
where the professor was always putting you
down, and that the other students were
mistreating you. You have admitted you have
a strong personality. Paige, do you think that
perhaps you draw the worst out of others?
I heard you complain about the same classmates at the university and how rude and
insensitive they are to you. Do you think that
maybe they believe you are out of line?

PAIGE
Out of line?

KAREN
Yes, out of line with them, so they attack you
in order to defend themselves and to get
even with you.

PAIGE
I cannot believe what you are saying!

KAREN
Paige, there is an old saying, "Some of us
may not realize it, but we are our own worst

enemy." Paige, are others really your enemy or are you your own worst enemy?

PAIGE

Karen, here we go again! You are just like everyone else I know, always picking at me and seeing me as the villain. I don't need any more of this!

KAREN

Paige, I am not your enemy. I sincerely like you and want to help you. Please, Paige, let's meet again when Olga and Natalie are in class.

PAIGE

(*in a calmer voice*)

OK, but back off a little bit! I am tired of your persecutory attitude toward me!

KAREN

OK, Paige, but remember, I am not in the business of persecution. On the contrary. I am in the business of making people happy and building them up, not tearing them down.

PAIGE

(*coldly*)

See you next week.

Blackout.

ACT IV

Scene 1

Lights rise. Olga and Karen are sitting in the living room.

KAREN
Good to see you, Olga. Please sit down.

OLGA
Hi, Karen.

KAREN
We already talked at length about your problems, and I gave you my interpretation of them. I have some suggestions for what can be done here, but first, let me ask you something. Did your mother display some of the same characteristics that you have?

OLGA
Oh, my God! Karen, you will not believe what I am going to tell you. My mother was obsessed with order and organization. She was a complete control freak. But what made it worse is that she was cold, aloof, and mean-spirited. If you did not do things correctly, she would not explain to you what you were doing wrong from her point of view. Instead, she would violently berate you, and she would just go on and on about it. The

more she berated me, the angrier she became. After her emotional tirades, I learned to clean the kitchen and refrigerator and put everything in perfect order. Then she became a different person. She would say, "Now Mommy loves you. You have been a good girl." It made me feel better, but they were just cold and empty words.

Olga stands up and paces around the room.

OLGA
I learned early in life to do exactly what she told me without hesitation, and I never, never questioned her authority. Her emotional tirades concerning order and cleanliness continued from childhood all through my high-school years. As time went on, I learned that the only way I could keep her off my back was to be like her. Even during my teenage years, I conformed to her incessant demands. When I was about thirteen years old, I realized that I was becoming just like her. Even some of my good friends would get mad at me and tell me I was acting like my mother. The only adults who really liked me were more like my mother.

Once I was out of high school and entering college, I got my own room. Unless I was around others or interacting with them, I just accepted myself as being that kind of person, an obsessive control freak. I was no longer troubled by it. Karen, as you and I both know, my nervous habits now control me. I do not control them. (*in a voice full of desperation*) Karen, I need some help, and I need it badly!

KAREN
I want you to go to the university and see a friend of mine, a clinical psychologist. I know her well, and she will be able to help you.

Blackout.

Scene 2

Lights rise. Natalie enters Karen's corner.

NATALIE
Well, Karen. I am here. I decided to see you again.

KAREN
Natalie, I have been thinking about you. Sit down. How did you get along with your father?

NATALIE
Thanks for bringing that up. My father is my favorite topic. He is perfect. I mean it, P-E-R-F-E-C-T. When I think back on it, Mom had a little resentment concerning our closeness. Dad and I did everything together. He called

me "my little princess," and I called him "my king." (*She stands up.*) Everybody at school was jealous of us. When I played basketball, he never missed a game. Well, I did not actually play that much, but when I became a cheerleader, he said I was the best cheerleader in the group. Dad would take me out to the finest restaurants in town. Just the two of us. He was the perfect gentleman, perfect in every way.

(*She sits down.*) Dad used to tell me if and when I get married, marry a man with high standards. He also said, "Make sure he is the type of man who will treat you perfectly and appreciate your absolutely fantastic qualities." Regarding people in general, he would drill into me that I should always keep my expectations high.

KAREN
Natalie, quite frankly, I think you should think about something. You love your father almost too much.

NATALIE
(*standing up, full of rage*)
How dare you say that!

KAREN
Sit down and listen. You want to be like him. You want to marry a man just like him. Maybe, or worse yet, you expect others to be

like your father. You have often said, "Perfect and with high standards."

NATALIE
What is wrong with that?

KAREN
Boyfriends and friends in general cannot, I repeat, cannot live up to his qualities and high standards from your point of view. You are not aware of it, but I believe that this is the basis for your problems. All of your love and admiration is for your father, so you cannot love others the way they need or want to be loved. Also, others cannot or do not want to have his standards for perfection. This alienates you from others. You have overidentified with your father, and this has caused your problems in the area of social maturity. This is sometimes a common problem with women. You can change your perception of your father and change your own self-image and still love him. At the same time, you can become a happier and fulfilled woman. My friend at the university has worked with many women with similar problems. I suggest that you go and see her.

Blackout.

Scene 3

Lights rise. Paige enters Karen's corner.

DENIAL, CONFRONTATION, OBSESSION AND RETURN

KAREN
Welcome to my little corner, Paige. Please sit down.

PAIGE
Hi, Karen.

KAREN
Based on everything I know about you, I don't think your feelings of persecution and personality problems go back to childhood. Your aunt, the one you told me about, was kind of that way. So when you say you inherited some of her characteristics, I agree with you. That is just the way you are. But these feelings of persecution and suspiciousness are complicating your relationships with others and causing you a great deal of stress.

Paige begins to cry.

KAREN
You can't change completely. Simply accept that you can bring out the worst in people. Reflect and become more aware of just how your defensiveness and aggressiveness is affecting others and, consequently, their reactions toward you.

KAREN
You are not going off the deep end, but at the same time, you deserve to be more comfortable in your everyday relationships with

people you care about. Paige, I really do believe that the clinical psychologist at the university can really help you.

> PAIGE
> (*confused*)

But you said I don't need a shrink.

> KAREN

And I mean it, using your words. You do not need a shrink.

> PAIGE

Then why are you suggesting that I see one?

> KAREN

Because this woman is very skilled at teaching people how to establish and keep satisfactory relationships with others.

> PAIGE

Do you think she can really help me?

> KAREN

Yes, Paige. She is not interested in probing into your unconscious mind or your previous life history. I am telling you, Paige, that treatment is not necessary, but you need to be educated in interpersonal skills. This woman is very skilled in this kind of therapy.

Blackout.

DENIAL, CONFRONTATION, OBSESSION AND RETURN

Scene 4

Lights rise. Natalie, Paige, and Olga are sitting in the living room.

>   OLGA
> Girls, how do you feel?

>   PAIGE
> Great!

>   NATALIE
> Let's toast to it!

They clink their glasses.

>   PAIGE
> Did I play my role well?

>   OLGA
> You were unbelievably believable!

>   NATALIE
> We are such good actresses.

>   OLGA
> Wait! Do you think we should tell Karen what we did? I remember so well the day she told us she could not afford to go to Brazil for her field study. She looked so sad, so that day we planned to be her field study.

>   NATALIE
> We did a good thing. So let's be quiet about it and not tell her anything.

PAIGE
I agree.

OLGA
No, I have been thinking about it. Let's tell Karen what we did.

PAIGE
She will be shocked.

NATALIE
Or very irritated.

Karen enters the apartment.

KAREN
Hi, girls.

OLGA
Karen, we have to tell you something. We wanted to be the subjects in your field study because you could not afford to travel to Brazil. We decided to fake our personalities. We are very sorry.

KAREN
(*smiling*)
Thank you, girls.

OLGA
(*surprised*)
Why are you thanking us? Aren't you angry?

KAREN
I was planning to write my thesis and then an article for a journal, but then I saw that you were role-playing—that is, faking it. So I decided to write a play instead.

OLGA
Girls, she turned the tables on us!

NATALIE
What do you mean?

OLGA
We wrote the play for her.

Blackout.

Together for Eternity

CHARACTERS

ALESSIA, a woman in her early twenties
VITTORIO, a man in his late forties
FRANCESCA, a woman in her early forties
WEDDING GUEST

YOUNG BEATRICE, a woman in her early twenties
YOUNG VITTORIO, a man in his midtwenties
TODDLER ALESSIA, about two or three years old
BEATRICE, a woman in her early forties
POLICEMAN

LOCATION

New York City

TIME

Present day

GOYA'S PAINTINGS REFERENCED IN THE PLAY

#1—*The Duke and Duchess of Osuna with Their Children*
#2—*Portrait of Maria Teresa de Borbon y Vallabriga*
#3—*Portrait of Count Fernand Núnez VII*
#4—*The Last Communion of St. Joseph of Calasanz*
#5—*Incantation*
#6—*Majas on a Balcony*
#7—*Saturn Devouring One of His Children*
#8—*Manola (La Leocadia)*
#9—*Savages Cutting a Woman's Throat*
#10—*Witches Sabbath*
#11—*El Tiempo de las Viejas*
#12—*Asmodea*

ACT I

Scene 1

Lights rise. Alessia enters Vittorio's penthouse. She drops her suitcase, and they embrace.

VITTORIO
Welcome home, my talented daughter.

ALESSIA
Talented? Dad, you are the renowned artist. I am not.

VITTORIO
According to your professors, you were the best student in the class!

ALESSIA
(*kissing her dad on the cheek*)
Like father, like daughter. Now I need to find a job and an apartment.

VITTORIO
Please, stay here with me. This penthouse seems so big since your mother died. Besides, I am gone most of the time at art conferences. You can use my studio. I don't paint as much as I used to.

ALESSIA
If I am not in your way, then I will stay here. Thanks. Daddy, remember when I was little, and we spent hours painting in the studio?

VITTORIO
I knew you had talent. You painted children like in Francisco de Goya's paintings.

ALESSIA
(*smiling*)
Yes, I remember.

#1—Background painting onstage, *The Duke and Duchess of Osuna with Their Children*

VITTORIO
You loved the duke—

ALESSIA
(*interrupting*)
Of Osuna. I remember how Goya painted the duke bending slightly forward as though he were protecting his eldest daughter.

VITTORIO
I remember how you laughed when you were painting their black pupils. By the way, any boyfriends?

ALESSIA
No, I have not found anybody yet. The girls at the dorm used to say I needed a man just like you.

> **VITTORIO**
> (smiling)
> I am leaving for England next week to speak at a conference on Goya.
>
> **ALESSIA**
> Oh, Dad. He is still my favorite painter. Just like you.

Blackout.

Scene 2

Lights rise. Alessia is painting at an easel in the studio. Vittorio enters and hugs her.

> **VITTORIO**
> How is my beautiful girl?
>
> **ALESSIA**
> (*kissing him*)
> Fine. Look what I am painting.

Vittorio walks toward the easel.

#2—Background painting onstage, *Portrait of Maria Teresa de Borbon y Vallabriga*

> **VITTORIO**
> Let me see…Beautiful! The face is perfect. Alessia, you are one of the best. Better than your father.

ALESSIA
Thanks, Dad. I like to paint happy people. If anybody sees my paintings, I want them to feel good. Dad, look at this one!

#3—Background painting onstage, *Portrait of Count Fernand Núñez VII*

VITTORIO
(*holding the canvas*)
Let me see…Look at the mixtures of gray, black, and yellow. Those are characteristic of Goya. Look at the whites of the tie, the frill of the shirt, and the right leg together with black, enhanced by…Alessia, you painted my face in the picture!

ALESSIA
I like your face, Dad. Let me show you another one.

#4—Background painting onstage, *The Last Communion of St. Joseph of Calasanz*

VITTORIO
(*laughing*)
My goodness, Alessia. You turned me into a priest.

ALESSIA
No, Dad, you are San Jose!

VITTORIO
Good job, Alessia. But now, I am a saint?

> ALESSIA
> Yes, you are. Let's go for dinner to our little place.

Blackout.

Scene 3

Lights rise. Vittorio and Alessia are sitting at a restaurant. Vittorio looks serious.

> VITTORIO
> Alessia, I have noticed that in most of your paintings there are three people: Francisco de Goya, yourself, and me. You have so much talent and imagination. Why don't you paint something else? Get out of the study. See something else. Let Francisco de Goya rest for a little while.

> ALESSIA
> I am attached to him.

> VITTORIO
> (*laughing*)
> And now you are drinking red wine, like he did.

> ALESSIA
> Yes, Francisco.

Blackout.

Scene 4

Lights rise. A few months later at the same restaurant. Vittorio and Alessia are having dinner and laughing. Francesa approaches the table and greets Vittorio with kisses on both cheeks.

                FRANCESCA
Vittorio! How are you? I have not seen you since you gave a conference on Goya's *Los Caprichos*.

                VITTORIO
              (*standing up*)
Francesca, it is good to see you. Please sit down. Let me introduce you to my daughter, Alessia.

                FRANCESCA
            (*extending her hand warmly*)
It is so good to meet you. You are getting quite a reputation as a painter.

                ALESSIA
            (*polite, but cold*)
Nice to meet you, Francesca.

                FRANCESCA
Your father is such a good friend. By the way, there is going to be a private exhibit of Magritte next week. Perhaps we can have dinner afterward.

                VITTORIO
How sweet of you. I definitely will be there.

DENIAL, CONFRONTATION, OBSESSION AND RETURN

> ALESSIA
> (*mumbling*)
> Boy, she is really making a move on him.

Blackout.

Scene 5

Lights rise. The stage is almost dark. Alessia is painting in the study. Vittorio enters.

> VITTORIO
> How is my darling daughter today?

> ALESSIA
> (*coldly*)
> Fine. How are you?

> VITTORIO
> Are you sure you are OK?

#5—Background painting onstage, *Incantation*

> ALESSIA
> (*still very cold*)
> Yes, I am fine, but these damn paintings! I just can't get them right.

Vittorio picks up some canvases from the floor and examines them.

> VITTORIO
> Alessia, these paintings remind me of Goya's *Incantation*, where a group of witches sur-

round a frightened woman. One witch read the incantation by the light of a candle. Alessia, the figure in yellow is casting a spell. On whom? Tell me.

                    ALESSIA
I don't know. I just took the idea from Goya. I don't know what they mean. I just was trying something different.

Blackout.

Scene 6

Lights rise. Six months later. Alessia paints at the easel in the studio. Vittorio enters.

                    ALESSIA
Hi, Dad.

                    VITTORIO
I need to talk to you about something very important. I am getting married to Francesca.

Alessia angrily slashes black paint across her canvas.

                    ALESSIA
Fine, Dad.

                    VITTORIO
Let me see your other paintings.

DENIAL, CONFRONTATION, OBSESSION AND RETURN

He steps around her to look at her other canvases.

#6—Background painting onstage, *Majas on a Balcony*

> **VITTORIO**
> This is good, but you painted the woman on the right like a prostitute. Alessia! The face looks just like Francesca. (*raising his voice*) What is wrong with you? Where is the wonderful artist who wanted to paint happy people? Your paintings are morbid and disgusting. Look at that one in the corner! Saturn is a woman.

#7—Background painting onstage, *Saturn Devouring One of His Children*

> **VITTORIO**
> She is angry and violent. She looks like Francesca. She is eating off a little girl's head. I am disgusted with you.

He leaves the studio.

Blackout.

Scene 7

Lights rise. A few days later. Alessia's room. The stage is almost dark, except for a light only on Alessia.

> **VITTORIO'S VOICE**
> Alessia, where are you?

There is a knock on her door.

ALESSIA
Come in, Father.

#8—Background painting onstage, *Manola (La Leocadia)*

VITTORIO
Where did you get that dress?

ALESSIA
I bought the material and sewed it myself. (*smiling warmly*) Daddy, do I look like Goya's lover, Leocadia?

VITTORIO
You do.

ALESSIA
(*happily*)
Thanks, Dad.

VITTORIO
(*looking around the room*)
Alessia, your walls look like the walls in Goya's *House of the Deaf Man*.

ALESSIA
What do you mean, Dad?

VITTORIO
The paintings are like Goya's *Black Paintings*. So dark and gloomy. Alessia, some females

look like you, but the grotesque females look like Francesca.

                    ALESSIA
                    (*smiling*)
I did not notice that, Dad.

Blackout.

Scene 8

Lights rise only on Alessia. Alessia is painting in the studio. Vittorio enters, smiling.

                    VITTORIO
Alessia, I have wonderful news for you!

                    ALESSIA
                    (*mumbling*)
I hope you dropped Francesca.

                    VITTORIO
You have been invited to have your own exhibit at the museum. Get your best work ready.

                    ALESSIA
                    (*surprised*)
Yes, Dad. I don't believe it!

Blackout.

Scene 9

Lights rise. Vittorio and Alessia are at the gallery.

                VITTORIO
Alessia, I see some of the paintings you had at the studio are here at the exhibit.

                ALESSIA
Yes, but I have two others you have not seen. Come with me.

She takes him by the hand to a corner, where Francesca looks at the paintings.

                VITTORIO
Francesca, I am so glad you could…What is wrong?

Francesca points at the paintings.

                FRANCESCA
These paintings are despicable, abhorrent, disgusting…

                VITTORIO
          (*looking at the paintings*)
Alessia, for God's sake. What have you done?

                ALESSIA
             (*smiling*)
I don't know what you mean, Daddy.

Blackout.

DENIAL, CONFRONTATION, OBSESSION AND RETURN

Scene 10

Later that evening at the studio. Vittorio screams at Alessia.

> **VITTORIO**
> I have had enough of you! I can see that you dislike Francesca. You have never told me, but you have communicated your dislike for her with your paintings. I love you so much. Maybe I did not want to recognize your feelings toward her. Alessia, I have been lonely since your mother died.

> **ALESSIA**
> Daddy, I am here for you. You are everything to me. You did not like my paintings, Daddy?

> **VITTORIO**
> I ordered the attendant to take down two of the paintings.

#9—Background painting onstage, *Savages Cutting a Woman's Throat*

> **VITTORIO**
> Alessia, the face of the woman in one of them is Francesca.

#10—Background painting onstage, *Witches Sabbath*

> **VITTORIO**
> The other one, like *Witches Sabbath,* all the faces look like Francesca. Alessia, please

sit down. Tell me what is going on in your head.

ALESSIA
(*innocently*)
Nothing, Dad. I just paint what I feel and my interpretation of Francisco de Goya's paintings. You taught me everything about Goya.

Lights off and on to show the passage of time. A week later. Alessia enters the studio.

ALESSIA
Dad, please come see my work. All the ugly paintings are gone. Look at the new paintings of Francesca. Do you like them, Daddy?

VITTORIO
Yes, thank you.

He closes the door and leaves. Alessia locks the door.

ALESSIA
Yes, yes. I have to paint what I feel. The scenes are black. Now I can paint Francesca the way she is: aggressive and jealous.

She pours a glass of red wine.

ALESSIA
I better hurry because the wedding is coming up in a few weeks. I have to paint a wedding present.

DENIAL, CONFRONTATION, OBSESSION AND RETURN

She laughs.

Blackout.

Scene 11

Lights rise. Wedding reception at the studio. Soft music plays in the background. Vittorio smiles at Francesca and raises his glass in a toast.

> VITTORIO
> Friends, my lovely daughter, Alessia, has painted a very special wedding present for Francesca and me. Let's toast to my wonderful daughter! Alessia, please uncover the painting.

#11—Background painting onstage, *El Tiempo de Las Viejas*

The guests gasp after Alessia uncovers it. Alessia's painting shows only one lady, old and toothless. She is dressed like a bride in a light gown.

> VITTORIO
> Alessia, what have you done? Remove that horrible painting from this room immediately!

Alessia is smiling as she takes the painting and leaves.

> VITTORIO
> (*looking at the audience*)
> Please, I apologize to my wife and to all of you.

WEDDING GUEST
A toast to the newlyweds!

Scene 12

Alessia's bedroom. There is a knock at the door. Vittorio enters.

VITTORIO
Alessia, everybody has left. I am tired and fed up with you! You are leaving this house tomorrow. I will rent you an apartment near the museum. I will provide for all your needs. You will not be welcome in this house again until I am convinced that you are the loving daughter I used to have.

ALESSIA
(*hugging her father*)
Francisco, don't send me away. Come live with me at *The House of the Deaf Man*. I love you. I will take care of you. You have been my only love. Please, come with me.

She cries and hugs him.

Blackout.

Scene 13

#8—Background painting onstage, *Manola (La Leocadia)*

DENIAL, CONFRONTATION, OBSESSION AND RETURN

The stage is almost dark. Two months later. Alessia lies on the floor dressed like Leocadia in the painting. She is wearing a long empire-waist black dress with a lace top and a black mantilla. She is surrounded by empty bottles of red wine and her own black paintings scattered all over the floor.

Blackout.

ACT II

Scene 1

Vittorio's apartment. Francesca and Vittorio talk.

> **FRANCESCA**
> Vittorio, come and sit with me. Please tell me what is happening with Alessia. Has she always been so attached to you? How was she when she was young? I want to understand her.

Blackout.

Scene 2

Lights rise. Young Beatrice and Young Vittorio are at the studio. Young Beatrice holds Toddler Alessia, who is crying.

> **YOUNG BEATRICE**
> Vittorio, please hold Alessia for me. She just won't stop crying.

> **YOUNG VITTORIO**
> Sure, let me help you.

She hands him the child, who suddenly seems content.

> **YOUNG BEATRICE**
> Look at her! She already seems more comfortable, and she has stopped crying.

YOUNG VITTORIO
Let's take her for a ride!

YOUNG BEATRICE
No! Whenever we go for a ride, she cries until you sit with her next to the car seat, and then I have to do all the driving. No, I don't want to go for a ride!

YOUNG VITTORIO
I understand. Let's stay home, and she will go to sleep.

YOUNG BEATRICE
Fine, but she insists on falling to sleep on your lap. You know what happened last night.

YOUNG VITTORIO
No, what happened?

YOUNG BEATRICE
She came to our bed and crawled in between us. She started pinching me. I told her she was hurting me. She smiled and then cuddled up closer to you. My friends tell me she is "daddy's little girl." I am concerned about this.

YOUNG VITTORIO
Why don't you call her pediatrician?

> YOUNG BEATRICE
> I did. He told me not to worry because she will outgrow it. I also told him about the frequent bed-wetting when she is not sleeping with us.
>
> YOUNG VITTORIO
> Yes, yes. Tell me what he said.
>
> YOUNG BEATRICE
> He said she would outgrow that, too.
>
> YOUNG VITTORIO
> Let's let her sleep with us. At least it is a temporary solution.

Blackout.

SCENE 3

Lights rise. The studio, ten years later.

> BEATRICE
> They called from school.
>
> VITTORIO
> Is everything OK?
>
> BEATRICE
> Not really. They said Alessia is disruptive in one of her classes and seems to bother the teacher. I spoke with the school counselor. She said girls her age go through hormonal changes and frequently behave in an im-

mature manner and may act out inappropriately. The counselor said they need patience and supervision. She also mentioned something about an Electra complex.

VITTORIO
I know that myth, but let me read more about it and see how it might apply to Alessia.

BEATRICE
There's more.

VITTORIO
Tell me, tell me.

BEATRICE
Alessia has a crush on her teacher. It has gotten so bad that I went to a group meeting today with the principal, the counselor, and her teacher. Alessia calls him on the phone at night. She is not a discipline problem in class, but they are concerned about the attachment she has to him.

VITTORIO
Have you spoken to Alessia about this?

BEATRICE
Yes, but she just laughs or gets angry. I will talk to her again, but you will need to do it also.

Blackout.

Scene 4

Lights rise. Six years later at the studio.

                    BEATRICE
          Well, Alessia is nineteen years old. She seems to enjoy college life, but I think she spends too much of her free time with you. She has boyfriends, but she says she prefers somebody like Dad.

Blackout.

Scene 5

Lights rise. Back to present day with Vittorio and Francesca in the studio. The phone rings. Vittorio answers it.

                    VITTORIO
          Yes? (*pause*) Yes, that is I. (*pause*) I'll be right there.

He hangs up the phone.

                    VITTORIO
          Francesca, I have to go. That was the doorman at Alessia's apartment.

Blackout.

ACT III

<u>Scene 1</u>

Lights rise on Alessia's apartment. Empty wine bottles are on the table. Vittorio enters. Alessa staggers over to hug him.

ALESSIA
Francisco de Goya, you came back to me!

#12—Background painting onstage, *Asmodea*

ALESSIA
Asmodea doesn't have to fly away because Leocadia is here with you. Francisco, please sit down. Have a glass of wine.

She serves him a glass. Vittorio takes it sadly.

VITTORIO
Thank you.

ALESSIA
Francisco, look to your left at my most recent painting. It is going to be a sequence of three paintings.

VITTORIO
Let me see...Number one. Alessia, Leocadia is saying something to Asmodea in this painting. Can you tell me what she is saying?

ALESSIA
Oh! Francisco, Leocadia is saying to Asmodea, "You don't have to fly away. I am happy now."

VITTORIO
(*examining the painting*)
Tell me, Alessia, Asmodea is pointing a finger at somebody bleeding to death. Who is that person?

ALESSIA
(smiling)
You know, Dad. Let me show you painting number two. Do you like it? Daddy, tell me if you like it.

VITTORIO
Can you explain it to me?

ALESSIA
Look, Goya is standing up with open arms. Leocadia and Asmodea are becoming one. Look, Dad, it is a synthesis of the two women walking toward Goya. Both women are smiling and displaying contentment.

VITTORIO
I see…

ALESSIA
(*drinking from her wine glass*)
See, Goya? You are letting Leocadia back in your life. Francisco de Goya y Lucientes,

DENIAL, CONFRONTATION, OBSESSION AND RETURN

look at the third painting. Close your eyes, Dad! Open your eyes. Dad, look at it! Do you see it, Daddy?

VITTORIO
Please explain it to me.

ALESSIA
(*holding a painting*)
Goya is sitting very happily and holding a precious little figure in his arms. The face is Leocadia's, but the body is of a child.

VITTORIO
Alessia, you can't let it go, can you?

ALESSIA
Why, Goya? I don't have to let it go. You will see why in my fourth painting.

Heartbroken, he starts to leave but turns around to Alessia.

VITTORIO
Before I go, come to the house and have dinner with Francesca and me next Saturday. We would like very much to see you at home.

ALESSIA
Thanks. That would be nice.

Blackout.

ACT IV

Scene 1

Lights rise on Vittorio's apartment. Vittorio opens the door to greet Alessia with a kiss on the cheek. She carries a wrapped canvas.

>**VITTORIO**
>Alessia, thank you for coming. Come in and sit down, please. What do you have there?

>**ALESSIA**
>Oh! It is the fourth painting that I told you I was going to finish. It is almost…Yes, it is almost finished. Let's look at it after dinner. Is that OK, Father?

Francesca enters the room.

>**FRANCESCA**
>Alessia, it is so good to see you! You look beautiful in that gold satin dress. The red wrap goes so well with it. You look like Goya's Asmodea.

They take seats around the dining table.

>**VITTORIO**
>A toast to my two favorite ladies.

>**ALESSIA**
>(*resigned*)
>Yes, two favorites.

DENIAL, CONFRONTATION, OBSESSION AND RETURN

>   FRANCESCA
> Thank you for coming. You look wonderful. Alessia, your father has gained some weight since we got married. We don't have to fight over him. There is enough of him to go around for both of us.

They all laugh.

>   ALESSIA
> May I have some wine, please?

>   FRANCESCA
> Sure. (*She pours a glass for everyone.*) Your father tells me you are quite involved in your art. He brags about how good you are and how proud he is of you.

>   ALESSIA
> May I have some more wine?

>   VITTORIO
> Yes, as long as you allow me and Francesca to take you to you home.

>   ALESSIA
> That won't be necessary.

Blackout.

Scene 2

Lights rise on the dining table, after dinner. Alessia is excited. Vittorio and Francesca sit at the table.

ALESSIA
Are you ready to see my painting?

FRANCESCA
Yes, we can hardly wait.

Alessia uncovers the canvas.

ALESSIA
Do you like it, Daddy?

VITTORIO
Yes, I like it. It is the balcony of the studio. The detail is beautiful. Let me see…Do you think the gray stone needs a little color? It also surprises me there are no people in this painting. You are exceptionally good with people and their facial expressions.

FRANCESCA
It is beautiful! Alessia, come to the balcony and see the flowers I just planted. You will like the color near the gray stone.

ALESSIA
OK.

DENIAL, CONFRONTATION, OBSESSION AND RETURN

> **VITTORIO**
> I will clear the table while you show her the flowers.

Blackout.

Scene 3

Lights rise. Alessia and Francesca are on the balcony at stage left. Vittorio cleans away the dinner plates in the dining room at stage right.

Alessia points toward something down below. Francesca leans over to spot it, and Alessia pushes her over the balcony railing, to her death.

A thud is heard. Smiling, Alessia walks through the doorway toward stage right, back into the studio

> **ALESSIA**
> Dad, maybe I can paint some of Francesca's flowers that are near the balcony. You said my painting needed some color. Can you come outside and tell me which colors you think would go well?

> **VITTORIO**
> Sure.

> **ALESSIA**
> Wait, Dad, it is a little chilly out here. Let me get my red wrap.

Vittorio crosses to the balcony at stage left. Alessia dons her wrap and follows.

VITTORIO
Look, Alessia, these flowers would go beautifully with…What are you doing? No!

Alessia puts her arms around her father's waist, and with a quick jerk, tumbles with him over the railing. A loud thud is heard.

#12—Background painting onstage, *Asmodea*

Blackout.

<u>Scene 4</u>

Lights rise in the studio a few hours later. A policeman examines a painting of a gray balcony, looks at the audience, and then looks at the painting again. He sets it down and notices a canvas attached to the back.

#12—Background painting onstage, *Asmodea*

He looks at Alessia's painting, and then looks at the painting of Asmodea shown in the background.

Lights off and then on.

The background paintings of Asmodea and Alessia's have writing scribbled all over.

POLICEMAN
(*reading aloud*)
Together for eternity.
Asmodea y Leocadia

Lights dims slowly.

A Return to the Beginning

CHARACTERS

PATTY, a woman in her early thirties
PREGNANT WOMAN
NURSE, a woman in her twenties
YOUNGER PATTY, a five-year-old girl
YOUNGER MOTHER, a woman in her midthirties
YOUNG PATTY, an eleven-year-old girl
MOTHER, a woman in her midfifties
PSYCHIATRIST, a man in his sixties
NEIGHBOR, a woman in her midsixties
SOCIAL WORKER, a woman in her forties
BABY GIRL, a few months old
SUSAN, a woman in her early thirties

LOCATION

Small town in Iowa

TIME

Present day

ACT I

Scene 1

Lights rise in the ward of a mental hospital. Patty is sitting near a window next to a pregnant woman. Patty rests her head on the pregnant woman's abdomen.

A nurse enters with a cup of water and pills on a tray.

NURSE
Patty, take your medicine.

Patty stares into space and does not answer. The nurse puts the medicine in Patty's mouth and gives her a sip of water. Patty continues to stare into space.

Blackout.

Scene 2

Lights rise. Younger Patty is at her mother's home.

YOUNGER PATTY
Mommy, why can't I go to school? The other children in town get to go.

YOUNGER MOTHER
I can teach you here at home.

YOUNGER PATTY
But I want friends, Mommy!

> YOUNGER MOTHER
> I can be your friend.

> YOUNGER PATTY
> But you are old. I want friends my age, like my cousin, Susan.

> YOUNGER MOTHER
> Susan's family moved away.

> YOUNGER PATTY
> If I went to school, I would have friends Susan's age.

> YOUNGER MOTHER
> Patty, the world is full of bad people. I don't want anything bad to happen to you. What would I do without you? You are my only friend.

> YOUNGER PATTY
> OK, Mommy. You are my only friend, too.

While her mother walks around doing chores, younger Patty holds onto the hem of her dress.

The lights dim and then rise to show a passage of time.

Mother putters around the house, with Young Patty holding onto her arm.

> YOUNG PATTY
> Mommy, I like being around you all the time.

DENIAL, CONFRONTATION, OBSESSION AND RETURN

> MOTHER
> (*kissing her cheek*)
> Good, we are a team.
>
> YOUNG PATTY
> Mommy, where is Dad? I have never seen him.
>
> MOTHER
> After you were born, he said I only had time for you, so he left.
>
> YOUNG PATTY
> I am glad he left. I don't have to share you with anybody else.

Blackout.

Scene 3

Lights rise. Patty and a psychiatrist are in his office at the mental hospital.

> PSYCHIATRIST
> Patty, what can you tell me about your life when you were a child?
>
> PATTY
> My mother was my only friend. We did everything together. She used to say that we were close friends. I guess we were codependent.

PSYCHIATRIST
(*writing on his pad*)
Tell me something about your husband.

PATTY
I think…Yes, I think I loved him more than he loved me. We were married for ten years, and then he left me. (*She begins to cry.*) But he did give me the most beautiful gift that I could ever receive, my daughter.

Blackout.

Scene 4

Lights rise. Mother and Patty are in the kitchen at Patty's mother's house.

PATTY
Mom, I am in love. I am getting married. Please do not worry. I am not leaving you. The house next door is for sale. We are buying it.

MOTHER
Well, that is fine, but are you sure that we will always be together?

PATTY
Yes, Mom. I am getting married, but we will always be together, and you will always be my closest friend.

Blackout.

DENIAL, CONFRONTATION, OBSESSION AND RETURN

Scene 5

Lights rise. Mother and Patty are in the mother's living room a few years later.

PATTY
Mom, my husband left me. I am sad because I really did love him.

MOTHER
What happened? I thought you two were happy together.

PATTY
He was in love with…

MOTHER
With whom?

PATTY
With the bottle. He was an alcoholic. I never told you. The only good thing is that I am pregnant.

MOTHER
We will take care of the baby. Come live with me. We will be a team, just like when you were growing up.

PATTY
Yes, Mommy. I will take good care of you, and you will be better soon.

MOTHER
Leave that house. It is full of bad memories. Close the house up, and bury the memory of the bad experiences inside. They will fade in time. Come live with me now.

PATTY
Yes, Mommy. I will come to live with you. I will help you around the house, and soon you will be well. Now that I think about, I don't think I will miss my husband that much. He was gone most of the time, anyway.

MOTHER
I understand.

PATTY
Mommy, I will take good care of you. If something were to happen to you, I just don't know how I could go on living.

She hugs her mother.

MOTHER
You are the perfect daughter. Knowing that I am going to have you here, I already feel better.

Blackout.

DENIAL, CONFRONTATION, OBSESSION AND RETURN

<u>Scene 6</u>

Lights rise on the mother's living room. Patty paces the floor, distraught. The cry of a baby is heard.

                PATTY
Mommy, why did you have to die? I miss you so much! I feel abandoned. You always said we were a team. Yes, Mommy, a team! You are gone. I am so alone and full of sadness. I have no hope for the future. Part of me is gone, and you took it away, Mommy. Mommy, (*crying*) I miss you terribly. I cannot get you back. Mommy, Mommy, the moment you left, my soul went with you. Do you know how I feel? I feel that I am at the edge of an abyss…Everything is dark.

Blackout.

<u>Scene 7</u>

Lights rise at the office of a social worker, who is talking to a neighbor of Patty's seated in front of the desk.

                NEIGHBOR
The mother and daughter kept to themselves. Very nice people: quiet, neat, polite. They never bothered anyone. The daughter, Patty, lives in the mother's house.

              SOCIAL WORKER
                  (*writing*)
And the mother?

NEIGHBOR
She died a short time ago. Patty has a baby. The baby is just a few months old. What really concerned me was the mailbox was overflowing with mail. Several newspapers were scattered on the front porch. These people were always very neat. I became so concerned that I decided to go to the house. I knocked on the front door, and nobody answered. The next day I went to their house and knocked on the door again. Still, nobody answered, so I went around to the back of the house and peeked into the kitchen window. I saw Patty lying on the floor by the baby. At first, I thought they were dead. I was ready to call 911, but then I heard Patty crying and begging the baby to feed her and hold her. I decided to call Family Services. I was referred to you. That is why I am here.

SOCIAL WORKER
Thank you very much. We will investigate the situation immediately.

Blackout.

<u>Scene 8</u>

Lights rise at the psychiatrist's office at the mental hospital.

PSYCHIATRIST
Patty, you are looking better today. I am going to continue to help you, but you also have to help me.

DENIAL, CONFRONTATION, OBSESSION AND RETURN

PATTY
Yes, Doctor. I miss my baby so much.

PSYCHIATRIST
The authorities had to take your baby away from you. It was brought to their attention that you were putting the baby on the floor and lying down beside her.

PATTY
I don't remember doing that!

PSYCHIATRIST
The social worker checked out your neighbor's report to make sure she was telling the truth. She went to your house and saw the same thing your neighbor saw. She said that she could hear your voice, but it sounded like a child's voice. She stood there for almost an hour and heard your childish voice over and over, begging your baby to feed you and hold you in her arms. Now, Patty, this is why we had to temporarily take the baby away from you. Don't worry, she is in good hands.

PATTY
Please, Doctor, I want my baby back right now. Then I will be fine.

PSYCHIATRIST
Patty, when you were with the baby, she was not OK. What you were doing could eventu-

ally be bad for her development and health in general.

PATTY
Doctor, I don't remember all of those things that the neighbor and the social worker told you. I love and take good care of my baby. On one occasion, I guess I woke up from a nap with my baby by my side on a soft blanket. I guess I just fell asleep with my baby on the floor rather than on the bed. What is so bad about that, Doctor?

PSYCHIATRIST
Patty, this is more serious than what you think. Why would you beg your own baby to feed you and hold you in her arms?

PATTY
I didn't do that!

PSYCHIATRIST
This is what concerns us, Patty. The fact that you do not recall these episodes. They did in fact occur on several occasions. These episodes were witnessed by your neighbor and the social worker. Patty, in some peculiar way, you were acting as though you were the baby and the baby was your mother.

PATTY
(*nervous*)
Doctor, that is absurd! I know that I am the mother and she is my little baby.

DENIAL, CONFRONTATION, OBSESSION AND RETURN

PSYCHIATRIST
But during these episodes, when you were lying on the floor beside the baby, for some reason, you became the baby and the baby became your mother. Patty, this is what we call oral regression and overidentification. In a way, your mind is playing tricks on you so you can get back what you lost. You don't recall these incidents because you don't understand what is causing them. Patty, another thing that has concerned me is a report that I received from the nurses on your ward. They said when you were first admitted to the hospital that you would sit by a pregnant woman and put your head on her abdomen. Patty, we need to work this out.

PATTY
I don't remember doing that.

PSYCHIATRIST
When we do, you can get your baby back.

PATTY
Oh, thank you. I will try my very best.

Blackout.

Scene 9

Lights rise. A light is only on the psychiatrist. The audience is a group of nurses.

PSYCHIATRIST

Thank you very much for coming. Your director wants me to lecture about a case we currently have here at the hospital. You are all familiar with Patty. I suspect that Patty experienced an intense, but satisfactory, symbiotic relationship with her mother. It is interesting that her psychotic episodes never occurred until her baby was a few months old. This was about the same time her mother died. Patty was evidently prepsychotic. She never developed a full-blown psychosis until her mother died.

These episodes were transitory rather than persistent. The psychiatric experiences evidently occurred when she would think about the loss of her mother. This was so stressful that she could not cope with the reality of the situation in a normal way, so her ego would regress to the oral stage of development. Then delusions and hallucinations would appear. Delusions are false beliefs or ideas about something. Hallucinations are false sensory experiences. In Patty's case, the hallucinations were visual. She would perceive the baby as a reincarnation of her own deceased mother. At the same time, oral regression and overidentification occurred.

The psychiatrist stops and points to a nurse, then cups his hand to his ear to hear her question better.

PSYCHIATRIST

Yes, overidentification is when the stressed individual identifies with both objects of a lost relationship. In this case, Patty is one object of the lost relationship and her infantile attachment to her mother is the other lost object. You see, she lost her own mother, and at the same time, she lost her infantile attachment to her mother. The only way she could get this attachment back was to go psychotic.

Blackout.

ACT II

Scene 1

Lights rise. Three months later. Patty is at home alone, holding her baby in her arms.

          PATTY
I am so happy to be home, but I am beginning to feel the same as when my neighbor and the social worker saw me. I have to be very careful. If I am not, they will take my baby away again.

There is a knock at the door.

          PATTY
I better hide.

Blackout.

Scene 2

Lights rise. A few days later. The social worker is in Patty's living room.

          SOCIAL WORKER
Please sit down, and let's talk. Patty, on several visits, I have found you on the floor making muffled sounds. The oral regression and overidentification have reoccurred. Now these episodes are lasting for longer periods.

PATTY
(*holding the baby tightly*)
Are you sure? How do you know this?

SOCIAL WORKER
I have been here several times. The kitchen door has been unlocked, and I came in and watched you. Sorry, Patty, we are going to have to take the baby away from you again.

PATTY
No, you are not taking my baby away! I take good care of my child.

SOCIAL WORKER
Patty, give me the baby!

PATTY
No!

SOCIAL WORKER
Do you realize that if I leave the baby here, marasmus may occur?

PATTY
I don't know what that is. I know that I am a good mother. Go away! Leave me alone!

SOCIAL WORKER
Sit down, Patty. Let me explain marasmus to you.

PATTY
I don't care what it is. Please, leave us alone.

SOCIAL WORKER
Please, Patty, listen to me. Marasmus is the gradual dwindling away of body tissues along with an increased susceptibility to various physical ailments due to improper nutrition and the lack of maternal love. I can see the baby has already lost weight. The baby needs proper social and emotional interaction.
I am sorry to say the baby is not getting it here. I must take the baby away again.

PATTY
I have maternal love for my child. She is my life.

SOCIAL WORKER
Patty, due to your condition, the psychotic episodes are causing distortions in time and space. You may get confused with time and how long you have left the baby on the floor. You may think you feed the baby regularly, but you are wrong. This child needs to be put on a regular feeding schedule, cuddled, and loved more often.

PATTY
(*crying*)
I love my baby. I love her.

SOCIAL WORKER
Patty, please give me the baby.

DENIAL, CONFRONTATION, OBSESSION AND RETURN

                PATTY
Will they take good care of my precious baby? (*caressing her*)

              SOCIAL WORKER
Yes, they will.

Blackout.

Scene 3

Lights rise on Patty's living room. Patty paces the floor.

                PATTY
I don't have the baby to help me. I can't lie down and talk to her. I miss the attachment to my mother. If my baby were here, but she is not…I wonder, was my baby my mother? I don't want to see anybody. If my neighbor comes over, I will play "not at home." The social worker asked me if I was lonely. I told her that I am alone, but I am not lonely… I think I am on a journey. Yes! Yes, I must close all the drapes as daylight bothers me.

She closes the drapes.

                PATTY
I like the darkness of night when it totally engulfs me. I sit in my comfortable chair. I grab two pillows and press them against my tummy. I can feel the soft cotton against my body.

Patty walks offstage and returns with pans of water. She sets them by her favorite chair, near the TV, then submerges her hands and feet.

                PATTY
I have to watch the reruns of *Baywatch*. (*to the TV*) Lifeguards, you are not necessary. Leave the people alone! If I could, I would jump through the TV screen and into the beautiful, clean water. I would need to swim fast so the lifeguards could not catch me.

A knock at the door.

                PATTY
(*screaming*)
Don't bother me!

She calms.

                PATTY
The darkness and the water covering my feet gives me such mental peace. I must get back. I am getting ready for a trip. My journey is starting. Yes, now I must get into the tub.

She rises.

                PATTY
When I feel the water splashing over my body, I experience such a wonderful feeling of elation and eternal bliss. It intoxicates me. I submerge my head and emerge only to breathe. In the water, I experience complete

DENIAL, CONFRONTATION, OBSESSION AND RETURN

exhilaration…beatitude. Sometimes I stay in the tub for hours.

Blackout.

Scene 4

Lights rise. The neighbor is talking to the social worker.

NEIGHBOR
I am very concerned. I have not seen Patty for weeks. The grass is overgrown, and the tree limbs are draping over the house like giant umbrellas. It looks as though nature has taken over the house. I fear that Patty has become so reclusive and withdrawn, she might be suicidal.

SOCIAL WORKER
Thank you for your information. I will call the police and ask them to help me investigate this. Is there anything else you can tell me?

NEIGHBOR
Years ago, a relative of Patty's used to bring her daughter to play with Patty. I believe they moved to a small town up north.

SOCIAL WORKER
Let me check her family records. Thank you.

Blackout.

Scene 5

Lights rise on Patty's bathroom. Patty lies in the bathtub, resting her head on the back of the tub.

          SUSAN'S VOICE
Patty! Patty! This is your cousin, Susan. Remember we used to play together and have picnics in your backyard. Where are you, Patty?

Susan enters the bathroom.

          SUSAN
What on earth are you doing in that tub with water up to your chin?

Patty glances at her.

          SUSAN
It's me, Susan. Patty, look at me. Get out of the tub. Come with me.

          PATTY
I am sorry, but I can't join you. I am getting ready to complete my journey.

          SUSAN
Get out of the bathtub. Let me drive you to your destination.

DENIAL, CONFRONTATION, OBSESSION AND RETURN

> PATTY
> (*speaking slowly*)
> The only way to reach my destination is by water. A car cannot take me there.
>
> SUSAN
> What do you mean?
>
> PATTY
> You will understand when we arrive.

Blackout.

Scene 6

Lights rise on the psychiatrist's office at the mental hospital. Susan is upset.

> SUSAN
> I just don't understand why Patty intentionally jumped into the river and drowned.
>
> PSYCHIATRIST
> First, Susan, tell me about Patty's last few hours.
>
> SUSAN
> Well, I finally got her out of the bathtub, and we went for a walk, along a river pathway where we'd play when we were kids.

Patty jumped over a rock wall into the water. I tried to grab her by the hand, but she swam away from me. It is odd to say, but she seemed happy. She had a faint smile. She went below the water, and...Why would she commit suicide?

PSYCHIATRIST
Susan, this was not a case of suicide. She had no death wish. Quite the contrary, she had a wish to experience life in an environment full of serenity and tranquility. Susan, in simple terms, she returned to the ocean of life: her mother's womb. It was the only way she could find peace. She experienced anxiety most of her life. We call this primal or birth anxiety. It occurs at birth, but a few individuals do not overcome it. Patty was one of the unfortunate few. What made the anxiety so extreme was the loss of her mother and then the loss of her child.
Susan, I know this is a sad time for you. However, Patty's external world was very unpleasant, particularly in her later years. Susan, do you believe in heaven?

SUSAN
I certainly do, Doctor.

PSYCHIATRIST
Well, you see, Patty is now in her heaven.

Lights dim.

Made in the USA
Middletown, DE
25 September 2015